Cynicism

Unveiling the Hidden Truths Behind Our Darkest Beliefs, What Lies Beneath Doubts, Fears, and Inner Conflict

JORDAN R. WESTON

Copyright © 2024. *JORDAN R. WESTON*

All rights reserved

No part of this publication may be reproduced, distributed, or transmitted in any form or by any means, including photocopying, recording, or other electronic or mechanical methods, without the prior written permission of the publisher, except in the case of brief quotations embodied in critical reviews and certain other noncommercial uses permitted by copyright law.

Table of Contents

Introduction 6

Chapter 1 12

   The Roots of Cynicism Historical Origins 12

      Psychological Foundations 18

         Social and Cultural Influences 24

Chapter 2 33

   The Anatomy of Cynical Beliefs The Role of Doubt 33

      Fear as Fuel for Cynicism 39

         Inner Conflicts and Self-Sabotage. 43

         Cynicism as a Protective Shield 48

Chapter 3 54

   The Hidden Truths Behind Cynicism The Illusion of Control 54

      Emotional Disconnect and Isolation .. 59

         Misunderstanding Empathy 64

The Cost of Holding onto Cynicism 70

The Mental Health Toll 70

Diminished Happiness and Satisfaction 72

Strained Relationships 73

The Cycle of Reinforced Cynicism 75

Breaking Free from Cynicism 76

Chapter 4 78

Deconstructing Cynicism Facing the Fear 78

Insecurity and the Need for Control ... 80

Releasing Past Disappointments 81

Embracing Uncertainty and Letting Go of Control 82

Rebuilding Trust and Compassion . 83

The Role of Hope and Idealism 84

Challenging Doubts 86

The Nature of Doubt and Its Impact on Perspective 86

Embracing Vulnerability..................94

Rebuilding Trust in Self and Others100

Practicing Patience and Discernment104

Chapter 5..107

Navigating the World with Open Eyes ...107

Cultivating Resilience Through Acceptance..113

Choosing Optimism Without Naivety115

The Dangers of Extreme Optimism and Extreme Cynicism 115

A Realistic, Open-Hearted Approach117

The Role of Healthy Skepticism 118

Embracing the Process of Change 119

Developing Emotional Intelligence121

The Core Components of Emotional Intelligence 122

The Transformation Through Emotional Intelligence 128

The Role of Empathy in Overcoming Cynicism 129

The Healing Power of Empathy and Compassion 134

Chapter 6 137

Moving Forward: A Cynic's Journey to Healing 137

Shifting Perspective 137

The Role of Self-Reflection................146

Finding Meaning and Purpose Again 154

Forgiveness—Letting Go of the Past 162

Conclusion 170

Introduction

Cynicism is more than just a skeptical or negative attitude; it is a belief system that has evolved through centuries, shaped by the collective experiences and harsh realities faced by individuals and societies. At its core, cynicism begins with a profound sense of disillusionment. It's the response to unmet expectations, the rejection of idealism, and the view that people and institutions are motivated primarily by self-interest rather than genuine goodwill. This belief system often emerges from experiences of betrayal, disappointment, or personal failures. It's a lens through which one sees the world—

distrustful, jaded, and, sometimes, detached from hope. But understanding cynicism goes beyond simply labeling it as pessimism; it's about exploring the root causes of these beliefs and how they influence both individual lives and broader societal structures.

The roots of cynicism can be traced back to the ancient Greek philosophers, most notably the Cynics, who rejected conventional society and its values. Figures like Diogenes of Sinope, who lived in a barrel and embraced poverty, showcased cynicism's radical departure from societal norms. For these early Cynics, the key to living a virtuous life was to abandon the societal expectations of wealth, power, and status, focusing instead on living in accordance with nature. Their criticism wasn't just about the failings of human nature; it was about the artificial constructs of civilization itself. Over time, this idea evolved, blending into different philosophical, religious, and political movements. Cynicism became less about rejecting societal norms for a return to nature, and more about exposing the hypocrisy and corruption of those in power.

Fast forward to the present day, and cynicism has taken on new dimensions. The modern world, with its rapid pace, constant information overload, and social media-driven discourse, seems to fuel cynicism at every turn. Political scandals, corporate greed, and the breakdown of public trust in institutions create an environment where doubt and suspicion thrive. It's not just that people distrust the government or large corporations; it's that they have come to believe that these entities, and by extension, society as a whole, are fundamentally driven by self-interest and power. In an age where news is often sensationalized, where information is filtered through biases, and where personal gains often outweigh collective good, cynicism becomes almost a defense mechanism. It's easier to protect oneself from disappointment by assuming the worst in others rather than facing the harsh reality of betrayal or failure.

The rise of social media and digital platforms has only amplified this. As individuals share their opinions online, often without accountability, the sense of collective disillusionment grows. We see the lives of others through carefully curated lenses, leading to comparisons and a belief that everyone is hiding something. The constant exposure to the darker sides of human nature, such as corruption, inequality, and exploitation, can erode one's trust in the goodness of others. In many ways, the digital age, with its fragmented and often polarized narratives, has created an environment where cynicism isn't just an individual's stance—it's a collective atmosphere. People are quick to judge, quicker to reject, and increasingly unwilling to look beyond the surface to understand the deeper forces at play.

But why, then, explore cynicism? What can we learn from this pervasive, often negative outlook on life? The purpose of this book is not simply to criticize or dismiss cynicism as a harmful way of thinking but to dive deeper into the underlying beliefs and emotions that shape it. Beneath every cynical thought, every jaded comment, and every disillusioned perspective lies a more complex, often hidden truth. Cynicism, when understood, reveals much about human nature—the fears, insecurities, and struggles that people face as they navigate a world that often seems unfair or indifferent to their needs.

By exploring cynicism, we can uncover the darker truths about society, but more importantly, we can also learn how these beliefs shape our perceptions of the world and, ultimately, our ability to change it. The book will peel back the layers of doubt and fear to reveal the human need for connection, understanding, and purpose. At its best, cynicism can be a call to action—a reminder to question the status quo, to challenge authority, and to seek truth in places where others may have given up. But at its worst, cynicism can breed isolation, resignation, and a belief that nothing ever truly changes. This book seeks to find the balance—to understand the role of cynicism in shaping our thoughts, beliefs, and actions, and to challenge it in ways that bring about a deeper, more empathetic understanding of ourselves and the world around us.

In a time when many people feel lost or betrayed by the systems they once trusted, cynicism can serve as both a shield and a barrier. It protects us from further hurt, but it also traps us in a cycle of negativity. By examining the roots of these beliefs and their manifestation in our daily lives, we can begin to untangle the complex web of emotions and experiences that shape our worldview. This book invites readers to journey beyond the surface-level cynicism, to confront the doubts, fears, and conflicts that lie beneath, and to uncover a more meaningful, authentic understanding of the world.

Through this exploration, we aim to transform cynicism from a source of despair into a tool for self-reflection and, ultimately, empowerment. By understanding what lies beneath the surface of our darkest beliefs, we can begin to navigate the complexities of life with a clearer sense of purpose, a more open heart, and a deeper understanding of what it truly means to be human.

Chapter 1

The Roots of Cynicism Historical Origins

Cynicism, as both a philosophical doctrine and a worldview, traces its origins to ancient Greece, where it was articulated as a radical departure from the conventional norms of society. The term itself comes from the Greek word *kynikos*, meaning "dog-like," and was initially used as a somewhat derogatory label to describe those who lived outside the societal mainstream. But in truth, the Cynics were anything but mindless rebels. They were deeply thoughtful philosophers who sought to challenge the status quo in order to expose its artificiality and corruption.

The first and most famous of the Cynics was Diogenes of Sinope, a figure who, through his eccentric lifestyle, became emblematic of this school of thought. Diogenes rejected material wealth and social status, choosing instead to live in a barrel or large ceramic jar in Athens. This radical form of asceticism, in which he lived without any of the comforts or luxuries afforded by society, was a deliberate rejection of the pretensions of wealth and power. Diogenes, in many ways, embodied the Cynic ideal by adopting a life that was simple, self-sufficient, and free from the constraints of societal norms.

Diogenes' philosophy was stark in its criticism of civilization, and his actions often carried a tone of mockery. He believed that true happiness could only be achieved by living in harmony with nature, unencumbered by the material pursuits that, in his view, only enslaved people. He famously wandered around Athens during the day with a lantern, claiming to be "looking for an honest man," a statement that mocked the hypocrisy he saw in those around him. Diogenes was not just a critic of wealth and luxury but of the very foundations of social life itself. He saw most people as slaves to convention, enslaved by the expectations of society rather than living freely according to nature's laws.

Alongside Diogenes, another foundational figure in the development of Cynicism was Socrates. While Socrates was not a Cynic in the strictest sense, his philosophy shared certain elements with the Cynic tradition, particularly his questioning of established norms and his disdain for the pretensions of the powerful. Socrates' method of dialectical questioning—what we now call the Socratic method—often exposed the contradictions in people's thinking and highlighted the flaws in their assumptions about the world. Socrates himself was committed to living a life of simplicity and self-control, and he rejected the pursuit of wealth, honor, and material pleasure. Though he did not advocate for the radical asceticism of Diogenes, Socrates' emphasis on virtue, wisdom, and self-examination laid the intellectual groundwork for Cynicism.

In the years following Diogenes, Cynicism became a more formalized school of thought, though its radical, anti-establishment ideals continued to set it apart from other philosophical movements. Cynics like Crates of Thebes and others further developed the idea of living a life that was in direct opposition to the materialism and luxury of the elite. They emphasized the importance of independence from society's expectations and argued that self-sufficiency and virtue were the highest goals one could achieve. For the Cynics, happiness was not something that could be found in external possessions or social approval, but rather in one's internal state of being—specifically, in cultivating self-discipline, personal integrity, and freedom from the whims of fortune.

However, over time, the meaning of Cynicism began to change. While it originally represented a challenge to the philosophical and cultural foundations of Greek society, it gradually became distorted. In the centuries that followed, Cynicism's focus shifted from its radical rejection of societal norms to a more cynical, skeptical worldview. The original Cynics were not simply disillusioned with society; they were striving for a more authentic way of life, one that aligned more closely with nature and reason. Over time, however, the term "cynicism" began to be associated more with negativity and mistrust. It came to describe a worldview that sees people and institutions as inherently self-interested, corrupt, or hypocritical—far removed from the radical idealism that defined its origins.

By the time of the Roman Empire, Cynicism had taken on a more individualistic, pessimistic character. The Roman philosopher Epictetus, though not a Cynic in the strict sense, adopted many of their principles in his Stoic philosophy. Stoicism, which shared Cynicism's disdain for material wealth and power, focused more on cultivating inner virtue and resilience in the face of life's challenges. But while Stoicism was practical and aimed at personal serenity, it was often more optimistic about human nature than the more jaundiced view held by the Cynics. Over time, the Cynic ideal became less about an active critique of society and more about personal withdrawal from it. The cynic of later periods often withdrew from the public sphere, believing that the world was too corrupt to be redeemed.

As Cynicism evolved through the ages, it increasingly became associated with negativity and a kind of existential resignation. In the medieval period, when faith and religious institutions were central to society, Cynicism took on a more religious critique. It often focused on questioning the motives behind religious authorities, accusing them of hypocrisy or moral corruption. In the Enlightenment and beyond, when scientific rationalism and individual rights came to the fore, Cynicism morphed again, this time into a critique of modern institutions—government, science, and the growing power of corporations.

In the modern era, the term "cynicism" has often become synonymous with distrust and negativity. While the original Cynics sought to expose the flaws in society in order to live more authentically, contemporary cynicism frequently manifests as a resigned disbelief in the possibility of positive change. Today, a cynical outlook is often characterized by the assumption that people are motivated solely by self-interest and that institutions are inherently corrupt, even when they claim to be serving the public good. The word "cynic" has, over time, become more a label for those who hold negative or skeptical views of the world, rather than for those who challenge societal norms with the goal of living a life of integrity.

Thus, the historical roots of Cynicism reveal a fascinating evolution. What began as a radical philosophical challenge to the values of ancient Greek society transformed over time into a more personal, inward-facing philosophy, and eventually into the modern sense of cynicism as a pervasive skepticism and distrust of the world. But beneath this evolution, the essence of cynicism—whether radical or resigned—remains a profound question about the nature of human behavior, society, and the pursuit of truth. The journey of Cynicism, from its philosophical beginnings to its modern manifestation, mirrors the shifting challenges and contradictions that humans have faced in their attempt to understand the world around them.

Psychological Foundations

The psychological underpinnings of cynicism are rooted in the complex interplay between human emotion, cognition, and past experiences. While cynicism is often seen through a philosophical or societal lens, its origins are deeply psychological, emerging as a defense mechanism against disappointment, betrayal, and emotional trauma. At its core, cynicism is a way for individuals to shield themselves from the pain of unmet expectations and the harsh realities of life. It is a coping strategy, albeit one that can, over time, distort the way one views the world.

One of the key psychological factors driving cynical beliefs is a profound sense of *disappointment*. When people invest emotional energy into something—a relationship, a career, a political movement—and that investment leads to failure or heartbreak, the emotional impact can be devastating. The deeper the investment, the more intense the disappointment. This sense of betrayal or disillusionment can lead to a form of protective skepticism. Individuals begin to question the reliability of others, the motives behind societal structures, or the integrity of systems that once seemed trustworthy. Cynicism becomes a shield, a way to protect oneself from further emotional harm. By adopting a view that "nothing is ever as it seems" or "people are inherently selfish," the individual preemptively guards against the disappointment they fear.

This protective mechanism is tied to an important aspect of human psychology: *trust*. Trust is foundational to human relationships and social functioning, but when trust is broken— whether in a personal relationship, a community, or in larger societal structures—individuals often experience feelings of vulnerability, anxiety, and fear. These emotional wounds can linger long after the event itself, and as a result, the individual may develop an increasingly cynical view of the world. If trust is repeatedly violated, whether by betrayal in relationships or corruption in institutions, the tendency is to start seeing all people and situations through the same lens of doubt and suspicion.

Beyond disappointment, *emotional trauma* is another powerful force behind the development of cynical beliefs. Trauma can take many forms— ranging from childhood neglect, abuse, or abandonment to the more complex emotional wounds inflicted by failed relationships or career setbacks. When someone experiences trauma, especially at an early age, their worldview can shift dramatically. Trust in others may feel unsafe, and the individual may develop a deep-seated belief that people cannot be relied upon. The world may start to seem like a hostile place, where ulterior motives are lurking behind every action. In this sense, cynicism can be seen as an adaptive response to the trauma of feeling powerless or betrayed. The person, having been hurt, starts to project that pain onto the world, developing the belief that others will always act in self-interest, just as they might have been hurt or abandoned in the past.

Cynicism also serves as a *coping mechanism* for feelings of helplessness or powerlessness. In a world where events often seem beyond individual control, where political leaders seem disconnected from the needs of the people or where personal aspirations feel thwarted by systemic barriers, cynicism offers a form of psychological survival. It allows individuals to distance themselves from disappointment by viewing life through a lens of skepticism. Instead of confronting feelings of powerlessness or frustration, the cynical person may dismiss the potential for positive change, convincing themselves that no matter what they do, the system is rigged, the people in charge are corrupt, and no effort will yield meaningful results. This belief, while it may protect the individual from the pain of future failure, also reinforces a passive resignation to the status quo.

This psychological defense also manifests in what is known as *self-justification*. A person who has been hurt may find it difficult to reconcile their ideals or desires with the reality of their experiences. To avoid confronting the painful gap between their expectations and the disappointing outcomes, they may embrace cynicism as a way to validate their feelings of betrayal. By adopting the belief that "everyone is selfish" or "nothing truly matters," they protect their sense of self from the internal conflict that arises when reality falls short of hope. Cynicism becomes a self-sustaining narrative—a justification for the anger, bitterness, and disillusionment that result from emotional wounds.

Additionally, *learned helplessness*, a concept popularized by psychologists like Martin Seligman, can contribute to the development of cynicism. When individuals repeatedly encounter situations in which their efforts to change their circumstances seem futile, they may eventually come to believe that no matter what they do, they will not be able to affect meaningful change. This learned helplessness reinforces the cynical belief that external events and the actions of others are beyond personal influence or control. It fosters a sense of resignation and detachment, where the person begins to see life as a series of unavoidable, predetermined events. Instead of feeling empowered to act, they may become emotionally numb, disconnected from the possibility of positive transformation.

Finally, *the projection of inner conflict* plays a significant role in the formation of cynical beliefs. Many people who struggle with their own unresolved inner conflicts—such as feelings of inadequacy, self-doubt, or fear of vulnerability—are more likely to project those fears onto the external world. If someone is deeply insecure or fearful of being betrayed, they may develop a cynical attitude towards others, assuming that everyone else shares the same flaws or desires to deceive them. This projection can distort relationships and interactions, as the person perceives the world as a reflection of their internal struggles. Their cynicism is not always based on objective experiences of betrayal but is, in part, an external manifestation of their internal emotional state.

In sum, the psychological foundations of cynicism are complex and multifaceted. They stem from deep emotional wounds, particularly those rooted in past disappointments, trauma, and the challenges of navigating a world that often seems unpredictable or unfair. While cynicism can serve as a protective defense mechanism, it also becomes a self-perpetuating cycle, reinforcing negative beliefs about human nature and the world around us. To understand and ultimately transcend cynicism, it is essential to explore these psychological roots, acknowledging how past experiences shape our present beliefs and actions. Through this understanding, individuals can begin to peel back the layers of cynicism and open themselves to new ways of seeing the world, grounded in trust, hope, and possibility.

Social and Cultural Influences

Cynicism does not develop in a vacuum; it is deeply shaped by the environment in which we live, including the influence of our families, cultures, and the pervasive media that surround us. These external factors play a crucial role in either nurturing or challenging cynical beliefs, often reinforcing a skeptical worldview or providing counter-narratives that offer hope and idealism. Understanding the social and cultural forces at play is essential in uncovering why certain individuals or communities are more inclined toward cynicism, while others may hold on to more optimistic or trusting perspectives.

Family Influence and Early Experiences

The family, as the first social unit a person encounters, has a profound impact on shaping the worldview of an individual. From an early age, children absorb the attitudes, values, and beliefs of their parents or caregivers, and these lessons can either foster or inhibit cynicism. Families that emphasize trust, empathy, and emotional support create an environment where individuals are more likely to develop a sense of security and hope in the world. However, when families are dysfunctional or marked by conflict, neglect, or betrayal, the seeds of cynicism can take root early on.

For example, children who grow up in environments where trust is broken—whether through parental infidelity, addiction, or abuse—may come to see relationships as inherently unstable and unreliable. This early exposure to dysfunction and emotional turmoil can create a deep-seated belief that people cannot be trusted and that emotional bonds are ultimately fraught with danger. The emotional scars left by these early experiences shape a cynical worldview in which vulnerability is avoided, and self-preservation becomes the highest priority. Over time, this attitude towards interpersonal relationships may extend to broader social structures, leading to an overarching cynicism about the world.

Conversely, families that emphasize resilience, communication, and positive conflict resolution can help children develop an optimistic and trusting outlook on life. However, even in these families, if a child is exposed to external events—such as systemic inequality, social injustice, or economic hardship—their sense of hope can be challenged, and a more skeptical perspective may emerge.

Cultural Norms and Societal Expectations

Culture plays a significant role in the development of cynicism, particularly in how societal norms, expectations, and values shape an individual's view of the world. In cultures where success is heavily tied to material wealth, power, and social status, cynicism often arises as a response to the harsh competition and inequality that these ideals perpetuate. When people are constantly exposed to the idea that success is the ultimate measure of one's worth, yet they struggle to achieve it, feelings of inadequacy and resentment can easily give way to cynical beliefs. People may start to feel that the system is rigged, that only those with privilege or power succeed, and that others are merely pawns in a game they have no control over. This belief, born of frustration and disillusionment, can lead individuals to reject the idea of fairness or justice, instead accepting a more jaded view of the world.

In cultures where collectivism and community are prioritized, cynicism can take on a different form. When the collective system fails to live up to its promises—whether through corruption, injustice, or inequality—individuals may begin to see society itself as deeply flawed. The betrayal of social contracts, such as a government failing to protect its citizens or institutions failing to uphold ethical standards, breeds distrust. Cynicism in these cases becomes a defense against the profound sense of disillusionment that arises when the larger system is perceived as incapable of living up to its ideals.

Moreover, the rise of individualism, especially in modern capitalist societies, can exacerbate cynicism. In societies where personal achievement is celebrated above all else, people are often taught to compete rather than cooperate. This culture of competition fosters a belief that others are rivals to be beaten, rather than people with whom to share common interests. Cynicism, then, can become a mechanism of survival—a way to navigate a world that encourages individuals to pursue their own success at the expense of others. In such a climate, trust becomes scarce, and suspicion flourishes as a means of protecting oneself from exploitation.

The Role of Media in Shaping Cynicism

Perhaps no external factor has a greater impact on shaping contemporary cynicism than the media. From television and newspapers to social media platforms, the media bombards us with narratives, images, and ideologies that often promote a cynical view of the world. The media plays a pivotal role in reinforcing the idea that corruption, deception, and dishonesty are not just widespread but inherent in the systems that govern our lives. Political scandals, corporate greed, and sensationalist reporting on social issues feed into the belief that the world is fundamentally flawed. This constant exposure to negative news, often presented in dramatic and sensational ways, can skew an individual's perception of reality, making them more likely to view the world through a lens of skepticism and distrust.

In particular, the way the media covers politics has a significant impact on the public's cynicism. Political scandals, lies, and betrayals become the focal point of media coverage, while positive, solution-oriented stories often take a backseat. This cycle of negativity leads to a growing sense of disenchantment with political leaders, institutions, and democratic processes. Over time, the belief that politicians are corrupt, self-serving, and untrustworthy becomes deeply entrenched, leading to a widespread political cynicism that can undermine engagement and participation in the political process.

Social media, too, plays a crucial role in amplifying cynicism. Platforms that prioritize sensational, polarizing content feed into tribalism and division, highlighting differences and conflicts over shared values. In this environment, people are often encouraged to view others, particularly those with opposing views, as the "enemy" rather than fellow human beings. The constant barrage of negative, often misleading or exaggerated information contributes to a culture of distrust. People become cynical not only about the political system but about each other—leading to a deeper fragmentation of society.

Moreover, the rise of influencer culture and the curated nature of online life perpetuate a sense of disillusionment. The idealized, often unattainable lifestyles showcased on social media can create feelings of inadequacy, leading to a belief that success is reserved for a select few who have mastered the art of self-promotion. The polished, edited versions of people's lives create a skewed sense of reality, which can lead to a deepening of cynicism, particularly among younger generations who struggle to reconcile these portrayals with their own lived experiences.

Challenging Cynicism Through Culture and Media

Despite the powerful role that family, culture, and media play in nurturing cynicism, these same forces also have the potential to challenge and counteract it. Cultures that emphasize compassion, cooperation, and shared responsibility can provide alternative narratives that offer hope and foster trust. In such cultures, people are encouraged to see each other as partners in creating a better world, rather than competitors in a zero-sum game. Media outlets that focus on constructive journalism, highlighting positive social change, ethical leadership, and community building, can offer a counterbalance to the negativity that so often dominates the headlines.

Similarly, family environments that promote open communication, resilience, and mutual respect can help individuals develop healthier coping mechanisms and a more positive worldview. Families that model forgiveness, emotional support, and an emphasis on personal growth can help break the cycle of cynicism that often starts with early emotional wounds. By addressing trauma and disappointment in constructive ways, families can help cultivate a sense of hope and trust in both individuals and the larger society.

Ultimately, the relationship between social and cultural influences and cynicism is complex. While our environment can certainly nurture and reinforce cynical beliefs, it also holds the power to challenge them, offering alternative narratives that encourage trust, hope, and cooperation. Whether through the values instilled by family, the cultural norms that shape societal expectations, or the media that informs our daily lives, these external forces are pivotal in determining whether cynicism becomes an ingrained worldview or just a temporary response to adversity.

Chapter 2

The Anatomy of Cynical Beliefs
The Role of Doubt

Doubt is the quiet instigator of cynicism, often creeping in slowly, like a shadow that grows longer and darker with time. It begins as a mere seed of uncertainty, a subtle questioning of what we have always accepted as true. Over time, if nurtured or left unaddressed, this doubt can grow into a full-fledged belief that the world, as we know it, is fundamentally flawed, deceitful, or inherently self-interested. The transition from healthy skepticism to deeper cynicism often begins with the act of questioning—the natural human inclination to seek clarity and truth. But when the answers to these questions are met with disillusionment or frustration, doubt evolves from a catalyst for learning into a belief system that colors how we see everything.

The questioning of societal norms is often the first sign of doubt. As children, we are typically taught to accept societal rules and values without question—what is considered right and wrong, how we should behave, what we should aspire to, and who we should trust. These teachings are passed down through generations, ingraining in us a sense of order and stability. However, as individuals grow and experience the complexities of life, especially through personal struggles or exposure to broader societal issues, they begin to question whether these norms truly align with their experiences. For example, a young person raised to believe in the importance of hard work and meritocracy might start to doubt these values upon witnessing systemic inequality, corruption, or a lack of social mobility. The societal promises of success and fairness, once seen as universal truths, suddenly appear empty, and the doubts about the integrity of social systems begin to form.

This process of questioning is not necessarily negative—it's a natural response to a world that often seems inconsistent or contradictory. However, when the doubts go unanswered or when the individual feels unable to reconcile the ideal with the reality, they begin to develop a more cynical lens. For example, the growing awareness of the corruption or hypocrisy in politics, corporate practices, or even within personal relationships can prompt a person to ask: *"If these people, who are in positions of power and influence, are acting out of self-interest or deceit, what does that say about the rest of society?"* The doubt extends beyond the particular issue at hand

and expands into a broader skepticism about the motives and integrity of others.

Similarly, doubt about authority plays a significant role in the formation of cynical beliefs. From a young age, we are conditioned to respect and trust authority figures—parents, teachers, leaders, and institutions. These figures are meant to provide guidance and structure, instilling a sense of order in our lives. However, when those in power are perceived as corrupt, inept, or self-serving, the foundation of trust begins to crumble. Political leaders who promise change but fail to deliver, religious institutions that scandalize their followers, or corporate leaders who prioritize profit over people—all of these instances foster a deep skepticism about the reliability and sincerity of authority. As individuals experience these betrayals of trust, the doubt that initially questions specific actions or policies begins to generalize into a broader disbelief in authority itself. In time, this doubt becomes the lens through which all authority is viewed, with the assumption that all figures of power are ultimately corrupt or untrustworthy.

Personal relationships, too, are not immune to the corrosive effects of doubt. At the heart of cynicism often lies a sense of betrayal or disappointment in others. The end of a meaningful relationship—whether romantic, familial, or platonic—often leaves the individual questioning not only the person who betrayed them but also the very nature of human connection. *"If someone I trusted could hurt me like this, how can I ever trust again?"* This is a central question for the cynical individual. The vulnerability that comes with relationships can lead to profound disillusionment, especially if the relationship was built on promises of loyalty, honesty, or mutual care. When these promises are broken, the emotional fallout can be overwhelming. Doubt creeps in not just about the person who caused the pain but about the very possibility of genuine connection. This kind of doubt can spiral into a general belief that all relationships are, at their core, transactional, driven by selfish motives rather than authentic connection.

The growing sense of doubt in societal norms, authority, and personal relationships often leads individuals to develop a worldview that sees the world as a place where hidden agendas and self-interest reign supreme. The doubt that initially arose from specific disappointments and questions slowly transforms into a broad, all-encompassing belief that most things in life are not as they seem. This belief system becomes self-reinforcing: the more a person doubts the sincerity of others, the more they begin to look for evidence to confirm their suspicions. As they find more examples of hypocrisy, dishonesty, or failure, their cynicism deepens, creating a closed loop of skepticism and distrust.

The role of doubt in the evolution of cynicism is not just about individual experiences but is also influenced by cultural and societal factors. In today's world, where social media amplifies both the positive and negative aspects of life, doubt is more easily nurtured. The constant exposure to scandals, betrayals, and injustices—whether through news reports, viral videos, or personal anecdotes shared online—serves to reinforce the belief that the world is full of hidden motives and unspoken truths. The online world, often dominated by sensationalism and negativity, makes it easier for individuals to fall into the trap of cynicism, as it provides constant validation for their doubts. This societal shift has created an environment where skepticism is not only common but often seen as a form of wisdom. It's no longer just a few individuals who question the world around them; it's become a collective experience, reinforcing the idea that doubt is the most rational response to the complexities of modern life.

Doubt, in its earliest stages, may seem like a healthy questioning of the world, a natural response to disillusionment and personal pain. But when left unchecked, it becomes the breeding ground for cynicism, a worldview that dismisses the possibility of genuine goodwill, honesty, and trust. What begins as a small seed of uncertainty can, over time, grow into a vast and impenetrable forest of doubt, where every action is scrutinized for hidden motives and every relationship is assumed to be self-serving. It is within this dark forest of cynicism that many individuals find themselves trapped, unable to see beyond the walls they have built to protect themselves from further emotional harm. And yet, even in this darkness, the seeds of hope and trust can sometimes be found—if only one is willing to question the very nature of the doubt that has taken root.

Fear as Fuel for Cynicism

Fear is one of the most powerful emotional forces in human psychology, and when it comes to cynicism, it serves as both a catalyst and a sustaining force. Fear of failure, rejection, or betrayal can significantly influence how people perceive the world around them, pushing them toward a cynical outlook. At its core, fear is a protective mechanism—a natural response to perceived threats. It is meant to alert us to danger, motivate us to avoid harm, and help us navigate a world that can, at times, feel unpredictable and unsafe. However, when fear is experienced repeatedly or when it is rooted in past traumas, it can spiral into a more pervasive and generalized form of cynicism. This form of cynicism becomes not just a defense mechanism against specific events, but a generalized way of viewing the world, other people, and even oneself.

The fear of *failure* is one of the most common drivers of cynicism. Failure, particularly when it is public or perceived as catastrophic, can leave a deep psychological scar. Individuals who have experienced repeated failures—whether in their careers, relationships, or personal endeavors—may begin to question their own abilities and the fairness of the world around them. They may feel as though no matter how hard they try, success remains elusive, and they are destined to be let down. This belief in inevitable failure can breed cynicism, leading individuals to view any future attempts at success with skepticism. The underlying fear is that no matter how much effort or passion they invest, the outcome will always be the same—disappointment and rejection.

For many, the fear of failure is closely tied to the *fear of rejection*. Rejection is a painful experience that strikes at the core of one's sense of self-worth. Whether it occurs in the context of romantic relationships, social interactions, or professional opportunities, rejection can feel like a profound judgment of one's value. When an individual faces repeated rejection or exclusion, particularly in formative stages of life, it can lead to a deep-seated fear that they are somehow inherently unworthy or flawed. Over time, this fear of rejection can evolve into a more generalized sense of distrust toward others. In an effort to shield themselves from future emotional pain, individuals may begin to distance themselves emotionally from others, adopting a cynical worldview that assumes that people are always self-interested, and that no connection or relationship is truly genuine. The fear of being hurt leads to the belief that it is better to expect nothing from others, as this shields them from the risk of disappointment.

Perhaps the most powerful and insidious fear that drives cynicism is the fear of *betrayal.* Betrayal is an emotional wound that cuts deeper than many other forms of hurt, as it strikes at the heart of trust—the very foundation of human relationships. Whether in the form of infidelity, dishonesty, or broken promises, betrayal erodes one's ability to trust not just the person who has betrayed them but also the wider world. When someone experiences betrayal, particularly from a person or institution they trusted deeply, it shakes their belief in the inherent goodness of others. The fear that this betrayal could happen again in any relationship—whether personal, professional, or even on a larger societal scale—can cause individuals to develop a cynical attitude toward everyone they meet. It becomes easier to expect dishonesty, manipulation, and selfishness because betrayal has taught them that trust is often misplaced.

The fear of betrayal does more than just alter one's outlook on relationships; it also alters how one engages with the world. Cynicism born out of the fear of betrayal often manifests in a profound wariness of authority figures, systems, and structures that are meant to provide stability and security. Governments, corporations, and even close personal relationships are all seen through the lens of skepticism. The individual begins to believe that everyone has ulterior motives, that everyone is out for their own benefit, and that no one can truly be trusted. This view is reinforced by the fear that, should they allow themselves to trust again, they will be hurt in the same way they were betrayed before.

Fear, then, plays a dual role in the development of cynicism. On one hand, it serves as a protective mechanism—a way to shield the individual from emotional harm. But on the other hand, when this fear is left unchecked or unaddressed, it can foster a more pervasive and limiting worldview. Cynicism rooted in fear not only protects the individual from disappointment but also limits their ability to connect, empathize, and hope for better outcomes. The fear of being hurt becomes a self-fulfilling prophecy: by expecting the worst from others, the individual often isolates themselves, reinforcing the very belief that others cannot be trusted or that the world is inherently unjust. In this way, fear, while originally intended as a safeguard, becomes the fuel that keeps the fires of cynicism burning.

Inner Conflicts and Self-Sabotage

At the heart of many cynical beliefs lies a complex web of inner conflicts, self-doubt, and unresolved emotional struggles. These internal battles often fuel and reinforce cynical worldviews, creating a feedback loop where negative beliefs about oneself and the world at large become self-fulfilling prophecies. Inner conflict, in particular, occurs when an individual's desires, values, and actions are at odds with one another, leading to a state of psychological discomfort and emotional tension. This dissonance can manifest in a variety of ways—feelings of inadequacy, fear of failure, chronic dissatisfaction, and a pervasive sense of disillusionment. Over time, these inner struggles can not only erode self-esteem and personal well-being but also shape the way one perceives the external world, particularly the motivations and behaviors of others.

One of the most powerful drivers of inner conflict is *insecurity*. Insecurity stems from an underlying sense of not being enough—whether in terms of abilities, appearance, relationships, or achievements. It often arises from early experiences of criticism, neglect, or comparison, where an individual feels they are constantly falling short of societal or familial expectations. This insecurity can manifest as a deep-seated fear of being exposed as "fraudulent" or "unworthy," which creates a constant cycle of self-criticism and self-doubt. When people are insecure, they may project their inner feelings of inadequacy onto others, viewing them as rivals, threats, or competitors rather than potential allies or friends. This mistrust of others is a cornerstone of cynicism—if someone believes they are unworthy of love, success, or acceptance, they are more likely to believe that others are similarly driven by self-interest or ulterior motives. The result is a defensive worldview in which people are seen not as genuinely caring or trustworthy, but as calculating, opportunistic, and ultimately self-serving.

Another key factor contributing to inner conflict and self-sabotage is *unresolved trauma*. Emotional or psychological trauma, especially when it is repressed or unaddressed, can fester beneath the surface, distorting how an individual views both themselves and the world. Trauma can take many forms—childhood abuse, neglect, bullying, failed relationships, or even societal marginalization. These painful experiences often create a sense of vulnerability, which, if not processed or healed, can lead to cynicism. Individuals who have been hurt or betrayed in the past may carry these wounds into future interactions, approaching new relationships or opportunities with an underlying belief that they will be hurt again. This fear of re-experiencing past pain leads to a kind of emotional armor—one that keeps others at a distance and closes off the possibility of deeper connection. In this way, unresolved trauma becomes a breeding ground for cynicism, reinforcing the belief that trust and vulnerability are risky and ultimately not worth the potential pain.

One of the most insidious manifestations of inner conflict is *self-sabotage.* Self-sabotage occurs when an individual unconsciously undermines their own efforts to succeed, often because they believe they do not deserve success or happiness. It can take many forms—procrastination, avoiding responsibility, pushing away supportive relationships, or choosing situations that reinforce negative self-beliefs. People who are internally conflicted may feel unworthy of success or love, and so, they unconsciously create situations where they fail or are rejected. The root of this self-sabotage is often the belief that, deep down, they are undeserving or incapable. These feelings of inadequacy can lead to a pattern of self-doubt, where every success is questioned and every potential for happiness is undermined by an internal voice that says, "You don't deserve this." Over time, this self-defeating behavior reinforces a cynical worldview—one in which life seems to be a series of disappointments, and the individual's efforts to change or improve always fall short.

Moreover, the feeling of being trapped in a cycle of self-doubt and self-sabotage creates a sense of helplessness that deepens the cynicism. When people feel as though they cannot break free from their own limitations or insecurities, they may begin to view external factors—such as other people, systems, or institutions—as equally flawed or untrustworthy. This deep-seated sense of powerlessness, combined with internal conflict, leads to the belief that there is no point in trying to change, because everything will inevitably fall apart. Cynicism, in this sense, becomes a form of resignation—an acceptance of the idea that life is inherently unfair, that people are inherently self-serving, and that any attempt at change or improvement is doomed to fail.

Ultimately, the relationship between inner conflict and cynicism is complex and intertwined. As unresolved emotional wounds continue to influence an individual's thoughts and behaviors, they lay the foundation for a cynical outlook on life. The process of self-sabotage, insecurity, and inner conflict becomes a way of protecting oneself from the perceived inevitability of pain and disappointment. But this protection comes at a cost—the individual becomes locked in a cycle of negativity, mistrust, and emotional distance, reinforcing the very beliefs that initially emerged as a way to avoid hurt. Over time, this internal battle deepens the sense of alienation and disillusionment, and cynicism becomes not just a belief, but a way of being in the world.

Cynicism as a Protective Shield

Cynicism, at its core, is often a defensive response—a psychological armor built to protect oneself from the wounds that come with vulnerability, disappointment, and emotional pain. Like an emotional shield, cynicism serves to keep the world at a safe distance, preventing the individual from becoming too invested or too hopeful in situations, people, or aspirations that might lead to further hurt. This defensive stance is not necessarily born out of a desire to reject the world, but rather out of a deep need for self-preservation in the face of past pain. It's a psychological strategy that seeks to inoculate against the potential for future emotional wounds by preemptively shutting down the possibility of trust, connection, and openness.

The most basic function of cynicism is its role in protecting the individual from disappointment. When people invest emotional energy into something—a relationship, a career, or a dream—and that investment is met with failure or betrayal, the resulting emotional fallout can be overwhelming. The sting of unmet expectations can feel like a blow to the heart, leaving the person feeling exposed and vulnerable. Over time, the individual begins to question the value of emotional investment, adopting a cynical belief that "nothing is ever as it seems," or "people will always let you down." This mindset is a way to prepare for the worst outcome, to minimize the risk of being blindsided by future disappointments. The idea is that if one expects the worst, the blow will not be as hard when it inevitably comes. In a sense, cynicism becomes a form of emotional insulation, designed to soften the impact of life's inevitable letdowns.

Cynicism also serves as a protective barrier against vulnerability. Vulnerability requires openness—the willingness to allow oneself to be seen, to trust others, and to expose one's deepest fears, desires, and emotions. For many, however, vulnerability is a source of profound fear, often tied to past experiences of betrayal or emotional abandonment. When a person has opened their heart to someone or something only to be hurt, they are less likely to make themselves vulnerable again. Instead, they erect walls of cynicism, shutting off emotional connection to avoid the pain that accompanies vulnerability. By adopting a cynical stance, the individual can guard against the possibility of emotional exposure, convincing themselves that relationships, trust, or intimacy are not worth pursuing because they will ultimately lead to disappointment. It's a way of protecting the heart from further injury by avoiding the very experiences that might require it to open up.

In this way, cynicism can become a form of *self-preservation*. The individual who has been hurt in the past may view cynicism as a rational, even necessary, response to life's uncertainties. It's easier to adopt a belief that people are inherently selfish or that success is never truly earned than it is to face the painful reality that life, at times, is unpredictable and beyond one's control. Cynicism allows a person to maintain control over their emotional world by limiting their expectations and guarding against disappointment. This control, however, comes at a cost: the loss of the ability to fully experience life's joys, connections, and possibilities. It can create a self-imposed isolation, where the person becomes trapped in a cycle of emotional detachment, unable to experience the depth of human experience due to the fear of being hurt again.

Moreover, cynicism can also prevent personal growth and self-actualization. When one is too focused on protecting themselves from harm, they may shy away from taking risks, pursuing dreams, or forging meaningful relationships. This self-protection can stifle ambition, creativity, and the willingness to engage with life's challenges in an open and fearless way. The individual may become stagnant, their emotional and psychological growth arrested by their own defensive mechanisms. Rather than confronting the fears and insecurities that fuel their cynicism, they continue to reinforce the very beliefs that keep them trapped in a state of emotional avoidance.

In relationships, cynicism can act as both a shield and a barrier. While it protects the individual from the pain of vulnerability, it also prevents the formation of deep, trusting bonds. When one is convinced that others are only out for their own gain, or that love is always fleeting, it becomes difficult to fully invest in meaningful connections. Cynical individuals often find themselves caught in a paradox—desiring closeness but simultaneously fearing it. They may push others away out of a belief that no one can be trusted or that opening up will only lead to heartache. This cycle of emotional self-sabotage can leave them feeling lonely and disconnected, yet unwilling or unable to break free from the very beliefs that protect them from emotional pain.

Ironically, cynicism, in its attempt to shield the individual from harm, can often create the very thing it seeks to avoid: emotional stagnation and isolation. The more one holds on to cynical beliefs, the harder it becomes to break through the walls of detachment and engage with the world in a more hopeful and trusting way. It is a protective mechanism that, over time, becomes a prison of its own making—one that keeps the individual safe from the pain of disappointment but also from the rich, messy, and beautiful experiences that life has to offer. The challenge, then, is not in the cynicism itself, but in the willingness to confront the underlying fears and vulnerabilities that drive it, to recognize that the shield is no longer necessary, and to learn to trust and engage with the world again, despite its uncertainties.

Chapter 3

The Hidden Truths Behind Cynicism The Illusion of Control

Cynicism, at its most insidious, offers the illusion of control—an illusion that can provide a sense of psychological comfort in a world that often feels chaotic and unpredictable. It's an emotional coping mechanism that, while rooted in doubt and distrust, presents itself as a form of rationality. In adopting a cynical worldview, individuals believe they have seen through the façade of human behavior and societal norms, and in doing so, they gain a sense of mastery over their environment. This illusion of control is alluring because, at its core, it promises predictability in an otherwise uncertain world. It allows individuals to believe that by assuming the worst in people and situations, they are protecting themselves from harm and disappointment. It's a form of psychological self-defense, where the belief that "nothing is ever as it seems" or "everyone has an agenda" creates a false sense of security.

The unpredictability of life—the randomness of events, the capriciousness of human behavior, and the complexity of relationships—can often feel overwhelming. From the whims of nature to the volatility of human interactions, the world can seem like a chaotic, uncontrollable place. In response to this uncertainty, cynicism offers a semblance of mastery over the uncontrollable. By viewing others as inherently self-serving or deceitful, the cynic believes they can predict the actions and motivations of those around them.

Cynicism allows individuals to feel as though they have cracked the code of human behavior: by assuming the worst, they feel as though they are less likely to be caught off guard or hurt by others. It's a way to safeguard against the unknown, to shield oneself from the vulnerability of expecting kindness, trust, or honesty in an unpredictable world.

In relationships, this illusion of control manifests as a desire to keep emotions at bay, preventing the possibility of being let down or hurt. Cynics often avoid emotional intimacy, preferring detachment or distance to the vulnerability of deeper connection. If they expect betrayal, rejection, or disappointment from others, they can justify their emotional distance as a rational defense against inevitable pain. In this way, cynicism provides a false sense of control over the chaos of human interactions. Instead of being open to the possibility of genuine connection, the cynic chooses to close themselves off emotionally, believing that this detachment will protect them from the inherent unpredictability of relationships. While this may seem like a protective strategy, it ultimately limits the individual's capacity for joy, intimacy, and meaningful connection, reinforcing the very beliefs that drive their cynicism.

On a broader scale, the cynic's need for control extends to society and institutions. In a world where political systems, economic markets, and cultural norms seem unpredictable and often flawed, cynicism offers an illusion of insight and understanding. It becomes easier for the cynic to assume that all leaders, corporations, or public figures are driven by personal gain or hidden agendas. By adopting this mindset, the individual feels as though they are better equipped to navigate the complexities of the world around them. They no longer have to rely on trust or idealism, which can seem naive or foolish. Instead, they place their trust in their own ability to see through the illusions and to predict the selfish motivations behind any action, thus maintaining a sense of control over what would otherwise feel like an overwhelming and chaotic world.

However, this sense of control is illusory at best. While cynicism may provide the temporary comfort of predictability, it ultimately undermines one's ability to navigate life with openness and flexibility. The more one leans into this defensive stance, the more one becomes trapped in a cycle of fear and distrust. In believing that the worst is always lurking beneath the surface, the cynic closes themselves off from the possibility of positive surprises, growth, and genuine connection. Life, with all its unpredictability, may seem threatening at times, but it also offers the chance for beauty, love, and change. By clinging to cynicism as a way to maintain control, individuals deny themselves the possibility of embracing life in all its complexity, both the light and the dark.

This false sense of control also extends to how cynicism shapes one's view of personal agency. A cynic may believe that the outcomes of their life are predetermined by forces outside their control—be it societal pressures, corrupt institutions, or the selfish nature of others. This belief can lead to a sense of helplessness or resignation, where the individual feels as though their actions don't matter because the world is inherently flawed and unchangeable. While cynicism provides a way to make sense of life's unpredictability, it does so at the cost of personal empowerment. By adopting a view that "nothing really matters" or "everyone is just out for themselves," the cynic removes themselves from the possibility of creating positive change or pursuing meaningful goals.

Ultimately, cynicism's promise of control is a double-edged sword. On the one hand, it offers a temporary shield against the unpredictability of life and the chaos of human behavior. On the other hand, it isolates the individual from the richness of human experience, robbing them of the ability to truly engage with life. The illusion of control that cynicism provides is fragile and short-lived, leaving those who embrace it trapped in a cycle of distrust and disillusionment. True control comes not from predicting or manipulating the actions of others, but from embracing the uncertainty of life and learning to navigate its complexities with resilience, openness, and hope. It is only by confronting the unknown with courage and vulnerability that we can break free from the illusion of control and discover the deeper truths that lie beneath our cynicism.

Emotional Disconnect and Isolation

Cynicism, while often viewed as a defense mechanism against disappointment and vulnerability, ultimately creates a profound sense of emotional disconnect and isolation. This disconnect does not merely occur on the surface level of relationships or social interactions; it seeps deep into the individual's emotional and psychological well-being, creating a chasm between them and their own feelings, their sense of self, and their connection to the world around them. Over time, this emotional isolation becomes a self-perpetuating cycle, where cynicism not only shields the individual from pain but also robs them of the capacity for deeper connection, joy, and meaning.

At the heart of emotional isolation lies the cynic's reluctance—or outright refusal—to engage with their own emotions. Cynicism breeds a distrust of vulnerability, both in others and in oneself.

Vulnerability, the willingness to feel deeply and to expose one's true feelings, is often seen as a weakness in a cynical worldview. Instead of embracing emotions like hope, joy, or even sadness, cynics tend to suppress or dismiss them as unrealistic, naïve, or ultimately untrustworthy. "Expect the worst," they say, because hope only leads to disappointment, and love only leads to heartache. In doing so, they disconnect from the full spectrum of their emotional experience, reducing their ability to engage with the richness of life. Without the ability to fully experience or express emotions, the cynic loses touch with their own humanity, creating an internal void that cannot be easily filled.

This emotional suppression also leads to a sense of disconnection from others. In relationships, whether personal, romantic, or professional, cynics often keep a distance—either consciously or subconsciously—to protect themselves from potential pain. They may wear a mask of detachment, making it difficult for others to truly connect with them. On the surface, this may seem like a way of protecting oneself from the possibility of betrayal, rejection, or hurt. However, in the long term, it fosters a sense of isolation. People around the cynic may feel shut out, unable to breach the emotional walls the cynic has erected. Relationships, at their core, require trust, openness, and mutual vulnerability—qualities that cynicism inherently rejects. When the cynic refuses to let down their guard or allow others to see their true selves, they forfeit the possibility of authentic connection, leaving them feeling increasingly alone, even in the presence of others.

Furthermore, cynicism can lead to a profound disconnection from one's sense of purpose or meaning in life. Cynics often view the world as a place of inherent selfishness and corruption, where self-interest reigns supreme and people's motivations are always tainted by ulterior motives. This view of life can create a sense of futility, as it implies that efforts to make meaningful contributions, whether in work, relationships, or broader societal change, are ultimately pointless. "What's the use?" the cynic might ask. "Everything is broken, and no one is truly sincere." This belief in the futility of meaningful engagement with the world leads to a lack of passion and direction. It's as though the cynic is standing on the sidelines of life, watching others live with purpose and conviction, but feeling disconnected from those experiences themselves. The more entrenched the cynical belief, the harder it becomes to imagine a life filled with authentic meaning or to feel invested in something larger than oneself.

As this emotional disconnect deepens, cynicism can also contribute to physical and psychological exhaustion. The mental energy required to maintain a cynical outlook—constantly scanning for signs of betrayal, disappointment, and hypocrisy—can lead to burnout. The cynic, forever on guard and emotionally closed off, may feel worn down by the weight of their own negative perceptions. Over time, this emotional fatigue can have serious consequences on mental health, leading to anxiety, depression, and a sense of existential despair. Cynicism, initially a protective shield, becomes a prison, isolating the individual not only from others but from the joy, fulfillment, and meaning that life has to offer.

The isolation created by cynicism also extends to the larger world. When one adopts a cynical worldview, it can be easy to start seeing society—whether through politics, culture, or global events—as a broken, corrupt system that cannot be changed or improved. This sense of powerlessness can lead to apathy, as the cynic may believe that nothing they do will make a difference. They become disengaged from collective efforts for change, viewing activism, social movements, or even personal acts of kindness as futile. This disconnection from the world at large further deepens the individual's sense of isolation, as they no longer feel part of a larger community or shared human endeavor.

Ultimately, the emotional disconnect that cynicism creates is not just about distancing oneself from others—it's about distancing oneself from life itself. By rejecting vulnerability, suppressing emotions, and adopting a worldview that dismisses trust and hope, the cynic isolates themselves from the richness of human experience. What begins as an attempt to shield oneself from harm ultimately leads to a profound sense of loneliness, disillusionment, and existential emptiness. The more deeply embedded the cynicism, the harder it becomes to break free from the isolation it creates. It's a cycle that perpetuates itself, as the cynic's worldview isolates them further from the very connections, emotions, and sense of purpose that might offer the path to healing and renewal.

Misunderstanding Empathy

Empathy is the ability to understand and share the feelings of another person, to put oneself in their shoes and see the world from their perspective. It is a cornerstone of meaningful relationships, fostering connection, compassion, and mutual understanding. However, for cynics, empathy can be a foreign concept, or at the very least, a difficult and often painful skill to practice. Cynicism, by its very nature, creates a lens through which others' actions are viewed with suspicion, distrust, and skepticism. Instead of seeing people's behavior as genuine, altruistic, or simply human, cynics tend to interpret it through a narrow, often negative, filter—assuming that others' motives are driven by self-interest, manipulation, or ulterior motives. This skewed perception not only distorts the way cynics view others but also undermines their ability to form deep, authentic connections.

One of the central ways in which cynicism obstructs empathy is by fostering the belief that most people are inherently selfish or self-serving. Cynics often assume that when others do something kind, helpful, or supportive, there must be an ulterior motive behind it. The idea that anyone would act purely out of generosity or goodwill is seen as naïve or unrealistic. In the eyes of a cynic, even seemingly selfless acts are viewed with suspicion, interpreted as attempts to gain something in return, whether it's approval, status, or a sense of moral superiority. For example, if a friend offers help during a difficult time, a cynic might wonder, "What do they want in return?" or "Why are they really doing this?" Rather than seeing the gesture as an expression of care or love, the cynic reduces it to a transaction, assuming that everyone is simply out for themselves.

This warped perception of others' motives makes it incredibly difficult for cynics to truly understand and relate to the emotions and experiences of those around them. If someone is struggling or experiencing pain, a cynic might dismiss their emotions, assuming that they are exaggerating, playing a victim, or seeking attention. Instead of offering empathy or support, the cynic may respond with coldness, indifference, or even judgment. They may be quick to label others' feelings as "overblown" or "self-pitying," convinced that people should simply "get over it" or "move on." In doing so, the cynic not only dismisses the legitimate feelings of others but also reinforces their own emotional distance, perpetuating a cycle of disconnection and misunderstanding.

This inability to empathize also impacts how cynics navigate their personal relationships. When someone consistently assumes that others are acting out of self-interest or ulterior motives, it becomes difficult to form trusting and authentic connections. In romantic relationships, for example, a cynic might struggle to believe in the sincerity of their partner's love or commitment, constantly questioning whether their partner's actions are motivated by genuine affection or by a desire to avoid conflict, gain something, or fulfill some other hidden agenda. This undermines the foundation of trust, which is essential for intimacy and closeness. Without trust, the relationship becomes more transactional than relational, and the cynic may find themselves emotionally distanced, unable or unwilling to fully engage in the bond.

In friendships, cynicism can breed suspicion and tension. A cynic might interpret acts of kindness or gestures of support as mere social obligation or self-serving behavior, never fully appreciating the selflessness behind these acts. As a result, their friends may feel misunderstood or unappreciated, leading to emotional strain. Over time, this can erode relationships, as others may become frustrated with the cynic's constant skepticism and inability to see the good in people.

Even in professional relationships, cynicism can create a barrier to effective communication and collaboration. If a cynic is surrounded by colleagues who are motivated by a sense of purpose or a desire to work toward a common goal, the cynic might dismiss their efforts as self-serving or motivated by career advancement. This can lead to a lack of cooperation, poor teamwork, and missed opportunities for growth and success. The cynic may struggle to trust their colleagues or see the value in collaboration, instead choosing to work alone or distance themselves from group efforts.

At its core, the cynic's inability to empathize with others stems from a profound fear of vulnerability. If they open themselves up to the idea that others may act out of kindness or genuine care, they risk exposing themselves to emotional pain and disappointment. To protect themselves from this possibility, they erect emotional barriers, assuming that people are only motivated by self-interest. This assumption, in turn, prevents them from engaging fully in relationships and experiencing the depth of emotional connection that comes from mutual understanding and shared empathy.

Ultimately, the cynic's struggle with empathy reinforces their isolation and emotional distance. The more they assume that others are driven by selfish motives, the more they withdraw from genuine emotional connections, trapping themselves in a cycle of disconnection. Over time, this lack of empathy leads to a distorted perception of the world and a deeper sense of loneliness. The cynic may come to believe that no one truly cares, that all relationships are transactional, and that emotional intimacy is either impossible or unnecessary. This, in turn, deepens their cynicism, as they continue to reinforce the belief that others cannot be trusted, and that the world is a place where people are driven solely by personal gain.

In reality, empathy is a key to breaking this cycle. By learning to see the world through others' eyes, by allowing oneself to be vulnerable, and by accepting the possibility that people can act out of love, care, or genuine goodwill, cynics have the potential to rebuild the connections that they have lost. It requires opening the heart to the uncertainty of human behavior and the inherent complexity of relationships. However, this process is not easy, and it requires a willingness to confront the deep-seated fears and assumptions that underpin cynicism. But by doing so, individuals can begin to rediscover the rich tapestry of human connection and the deep fulfillment that comes from genuine empathy and shared understanding.

The Cost of Holding onto Cynicism

Cynicism, while often appearing as a protective defense mechanism against life's uncertainties and disappointments, can exact a heavy personal toll over time. What begins as a seemingly rational and even self-preserving worldview can slowly erode one's mental health, happiness, and relationships. The long-term effects of holding onto cynicism are far-reaching and often insidious, subtly undermining one's emotional well-being, sense of purpose, and capacity for joy. The very traits that make cynicism appear to offer protection—distrust, detachment, and skepticism—can eventually become sources of deep personal suffering, creating a cycle of emotional isolation and existential dissatisfaction.

The Mental Health Toll

One of the most immediate and long-term costs of cynicism is its impact on mental health.

Cynicism tends to breed a pervasive sense of negativity, which colors the way an individual perceives the world and their place in it. The constant expectation of disappointment, betrayal, or failure creates a lens through which every situation is seen in a pessimistic light. Over time, this outlook can lead to chronic feelings of frustration, helplessness, and even hopelessness.

The emotional exhaustion that comes with cynicism can be psychologically taxing. Cynics are often in a state of hypervigilance, constantly guarding themselves against the potential for hurt or letdown. This heightened state of alertness, coupled with a fundamental distrust of others, contributes to elevated levels of stress and anxiety. Rather than allowing themselves to experience life's natural ebb and flow of emotions, cynics remain on edge, bracing themselves for the worst. This persistent state of emotional tension can lead to burnout, making it increasingly difficult to experience moments of relaxation or contentment.

Furthermore, cynicism is closely linked to feelings of *disillusionment* and *meaninglessness*. When individuals develop a worldview that sees people, institutions, and life itself as inherently flawed or corrupt, it becomes difficult to find purpose or fulfillment. Cynicism fosters a deep sense of alienation from others and a loss of faith in the things that once brought joy or meaning. Over time, this can manifest as *depression*, as the person struggles to find a reason to keep striving or engaging with the world around them. The absence of hope, combined with a pervasive belief that things will never get better, can lead to feelings of profound sadness and despair.

Diminished Happiness and Satisfaction

At its core, cynicism undermines happiness because it prevents individuals from fully embracing life's positive experiences. Life, despite its inevitable struggles, offers moments of joy, connection, and fulfillment. These moments, however, are often dismissed or downplayed by cynics, who have become conditioned to expect disappointment rather than delight. A cynic might attend a celebration or family gathering but view it through a lens of suspicion—assuming people's motives are insincere or that happiness is fleeting and temporary. As a result, they fail to fully immerse themselves in the positive emotions of the moment, instead holding back in anticipation of the inevitable letdown.

Cynicism also feeds into a sense of existential dissatisfaction. People who hold cynical beliefs often struggle to derive meaning from their experiences. When you view the world through the lens of distrust and disappointment, it's difficult to feel a sense of gratitude for what you have or optimism for what is yet to come. Instead of appreciating life's fleeting moments of joy, cynics are preoccupied with the notion that life is inherently unfair or that everyone is motivated by self-interest. This mindset not only dampens happiness but also prevents individuals from creating the kind of positive, rewarding experiences that contribute to a sense of personal well-being and fulfillment.

Strained Relationships

Perhaps one of the most damaging effects of cynicism is its toll on personal relationships. Relationships, whether romantic, familial, or friendships, are built on trust, openness, and a shared willingness to be vulnerable. Cynicism, however, fosters an environment of emotional distance and distrust, making it difficult for individuals to connect with others in meaningful ways. In romantic relationships, for example, cynicism can manifest as emotional detachment, suspicion, or a constant fear of being hurt. If one partner believes that all relationships ultimately end in betrayal or disappointment, they may withhold affection, become overly guarded, or sabotage the relationship in subtle ways. This can create a cycle where the very fear of emotional vulnerability leads to the breakdown of the connection, fulfilling the cynical belief that intimacy and love are doomed to fail.

In friendships and family dynamics, cynicism can similarly breed conflict and distance. Cynics may be quick to judge the motives of others, assuming that their friends or family members are only seeking personal gain or attempting to manipulate them in some way. This constant suspicion not only undermines trust but also prevents the individual from fully engaging with and appreciating the people in their lives. Rather than seeing others as capable of genuine kindness or selflessness, they are viewed through a lens of skepticism, where even acts of love or support are questioned or dismissed. Over time, this erodes the emotional bonds that hold relationships together, leaving the cynic feeling increasingly isolated and misunderstood.

The cost of cynicism in relationships is not limited to others; it is also a personal toll. Those who hold cynical beliefs often find themselves trapped in a cycle of emotional isolation, where they are unable or unwilling to open themselves up to the love and support of others. This isolation leads to feelings of loneliness and emotional emptiness, as the cynic closes themselves off from the very connections that could bring them joy, comfort, and a sense of belonging.

The Cycle of Reinforced Cynicism

The longer cynicism is held onto, the more deeply ingrained it becomes in an individual's worldview. As cynics encounter setbacks, betrayals, or disappointments, these experiences are interpreted as further evidence of the flaws in the world, reinforcing the belief that everyone and everything is driven by ulterior motives or destined to fail. This cycle of negative reinforcement makes it difficult to break free from cynicism, as each new disappointment serves as "proof" that the world is as bleak and untrustworthy as they believe. The more they expect the worst, the more they are likely to find it—whether in others' behavior, societal structures, or even in their own internal conflicts. This self-fulfilling prophecy locks the cynic into a perpetual state of disillusionment, where hope and optimism become increasingly elusive.

Breaking Free from Cynicism

While the personal toll of cynicism is clear, it's important to recognize that change is possible. Cynicism, like any defense mechanism, can be dismantled with time, self-awareness, and the willingness to embrace vulnerability. Breaking free from cynicism requires the individual to confront their fears, heal from past emotional wounds, and open themselves up to the possibility of connection and trust. This process is neither simple nor quick, but it is necessary for anyone who wishes to experience the full spectrum of human emotion—joy, love, and fulfillment—without the constraints of constant doubt and disillusionment.

Ultimately, the cost of holding onto cynicism is high, but so too is the reward for letting it go. By learning to trust again, to embrace hope, and to experience life with all its complexities, one can begin to move beyond the narrow, self-protective worldview that cynicism offers. Only then can the cynic experience the true richness of human connection, personal growth, and lasting happiness.

Chapter 4

Deconstructing Cynicism Facing the Fear

Breaking free from cynicism is not a simple or immediate process; it requires a deep and often painful confrontation with one's own fears, insecurities, and past disappointments. At the heart of cynicism lies a defense mechanism—a protective shell forged in response to emotional pain, betrayal, and disillusionment. While this shield may have once served a purpose, allowing individuals to navigate a world that feels unpredictable and unsafe, it becomes a barrier that ultimately prevents personal growth, meaningful relationships, and a fuller engagement with life. The first step in deconstructing cynicism is to face the very fears and wounds that give rise to it, and in doing so, to challenge the belief systems that have become entrenched over time.

Confronting Fear: The Heart of Cynicism

Fear is often the driving force behind cynicism. Whether it's the fear of failure, rejection, betrayal, or vulnerability, fear acts as a catalyst that drives people to adopt a cynical outlook as a way to protect themselves from further emotional harm. The cynical person, having been burned by life in some way, becomes hyper-aware of potential threats—both real and imagined. This heightened sense of alertness, while it may seem like a form of self-preservation, only perpetuates a cycle of emotional disconnection and mistrust.

To begin dismantling cynicism, one must first confront the underlying fears that drive it. This means being willing to explore the emotional scars left by past experiences—whether from childhood, relationships, or personal disappointments—and to acknowledge the ways in which these fears shape current beliefs and behaviors. For instance, if someone has experienced betrayal or abandonment, their fear of being hurt again may cause them to shut down emotionally, refusing to trust others. However, by facing the fear of vulnerability head-on, they can begin to separate their past wounds from their present circumstances, realizing that not all people or situations are destined to lead to the same painful outcomes.

Insecurity and the Need for Control

Many cynical beliefs stem from a deep sense of insecurity—the feeling that one is not enough, that one's worth is conditional, or that failure is inevitable. This insecurity often manifests as a need for control, whether it's control over emotions, relationships, or the outcomes of one's efforts. Cynics, in their desire to avoid disappointment, begin to control their expectations and emotional investments, often to the point of emotional detachment.

To break free from this pattern, one must confront their insecurity and the need for control that arises from it. This involves challenging the belief that vulnerability is a weakness and recognizing that emotional openness is not only a source of strength but also an essential part of the human experience. In confronting insecurity, individuals can learn to trust themselves more fully, accepting that failure, rejection, and disappointment are a natural part of life and that they do not define one's worth or potential. Through this process, they begin to rebuild their sense of self-esteem and self-compassion, shedding the armor of cynicism that has kept them emotionally isolated.

Releasing Past Disappointments

Another critical aspect of deconstructing cynicism is addressing past disappointments—particularly those experiences that have led individuals to adopt a worldview of mistrust and skepticism. These disappointments, whether they stem from broken relationships, failed dreams, or systemic injustices, can be deeply painful and difficult to let go of. The cynic often holds onto these past wounds, not because they want to be stuck in pain, but because holding onto them feels like a way of protecting themselves from future harm. If they expect the worst, they reason, they won't be caught off guard again.

However, while it may seem comforting in the short term to dwell on past disappointments, it only deepens the grip of cynicism. The past cannot be changed, and by allowing it to dictate one's present mindset, individuals are essentially allowing their past pain to control their future possibilities. To truly release cynicism, one must face these past disappointments, grieve the losses, and ultimately let go of the need for revenge, bitterness, or perpetual skepticism. This process requires emotional courage— acknowledging the hurt without allowing it to define the person's entire narrative. It involves understanding that while the past has shaped them, it does not have to dictate their future.

Embracing Uncertainty and Letting Go of Control

A significant part of overcoming cynicism is learning to embrace the uncertainty of life. Cynicism thrives in an environment where control is paramount—where everything is questioned, doubted, and analyzed to avoid disappointment or vulnerability. The cynic, in their desire to avoid emotional risk, builds walls around themselves, creating an illusion of control over their circumstances. Yet, this need for control often exacerbates feelings of isolation and anxiety, as it's impossible to control every outcome or the behavior of others.

Letting go of the need for absolute control can be liberating. It doesn't mean resigning oneself to passivity or allowing others to take advantage, but rather recognizing that uncertainty is a natural part of life. By embracing the unknown, individuals can open themselves up to new experiences, relationships, and possibilities that they might have otherwise closed themselves off to. This shift in perspective involves developing trust—not just in others, but in the process of life itself. It's about allowing space for vulnerability and trusting that, even in the face of uncertainty, the capacity for joy, connection, and growth is still very much possible.

Rebuilding Trust and Compassion

Trust is one of the first casualties of cynicism. The belief that people are inherently selfish or self-serving creates an emotional wall between the cynic and the world around them. Yet, to deconstruct cynicism, it is essential to rebuild trust—not only in others but also in oneself. Trusting others begins with learning to trust one's own instincts and judgment, and understanding that while some people may let us down, others will prove to be reliable, kind, and compassionate.

This rebuilding of trust is also closely tied to cultivating compassion—for both oneself and others. Cynics often have harsh internal dialogues, condemning themselves for perceived shortcomings and assuming the worst about others. By practicing self-compassion, individuals can begin to soften these negative internal voices and treat themselves with the same understanding they would offer a friend. Additionally, extending compassion to others—acknowledging their struggles, imperfections, and humanity—can help to counterbalance the cynical belief that people are driven purely by self-interest.

The Role of Hope and Idealism

Finally, deconstructing cynicism requires a reawakening of hope and idealism—the very qualities that cynicism has buried or distorted. Hope is not naïveté, nor is idealism a fool's dream; rather, they are powerful forces that help us imagine a better world and inspire us to work toward it. To break free from cynicism, individuals must allow themselves to believe in the possibility of positive change—not just in the world, but in their own lives. This doesn't mean ignoring the harsh realities of life, but rather choosing to believe that goodness, integrity, and connection are still worth striving for. It's about recognizing that while the world is far from perfect, it is also filled with beauty, kindness, and the potential for transformation.

In the end, confronting one's fears, insecurities, and past disappointments is key to breaking free from the cycle of cynicism. It is through this deep, often difficult self-work that individuals can reclaim their emotional freedom and restore their ability to connect authentically with others. By letting go of the protective shield of cynicism, they open themselves up to the richness of life— its unpredictability, its imperfections, and its moments of profound meaning and joy.

Challenging Doubts

Challenging the doubts that fuel cynicism is an essential part of breaking free from its grip. Doubt is the silent engine behind much of cynical thinking—whether it's doubt about the integrity of others, the fairness of society, or the possibility of personal success and happiness. It often begins innocuously, as a small question or skepticism, but over time, if left unchecked, it grows into a more pervasive belief system. The first step in challenging these doubts is recognizing that they are, at their core, just *beliefs*—not immutable truths. Through techniques like cognitive reframing and self-reflection, individuals can begin to question the assumptions that support their cynical worldview and reassess the way they interpret the actions and motivations of others.

The Nature of Doubt and Its Impact on Perspective

At its heart, doubt arises from a lack of certainty or a fear of being wrong. It's a natural and often useful human response to situations that seem ambiguous or threatening. However, when doubt becomes chronic or unfounded, it can lead to a distorted perception of reality. For cynics, doubt often manifests as a tendency to question the motives behind others' actions or the integrity of social systems. For example, a cynic might assume that a colleague who offers help is only doing so because they want something in return, or they may view a social initiative aimed at improving community welfare as nothing more than a façade for political gain. These doubts, though they may seem reasonable on the surface, often stem from a deep-seated belief that the world is fundamentally untrustworthy and that no one acts without ulterior motives.

This mindset, while protective in nature, is ultimately limiting. It prevents individuals from fully engaging with others or seeing the world with an open mind. By assuming the worst, cynics miss opportunities for genuine connection, empathy, and personal growth. The challenge, therefore, is not just to dismiss or suppress these doubts but to engage with them consciously, to explore their origins and question their validity. This is where cognitive reframing—a powerful psychological technique—comes into play.

Cognitive Reframing: Changing the Lens Through Which We See the World

Cognitive reframing is the process of consciously challenging and shifting negative or unproductive thought patterns. It involves identifying the beliefs or assumptions that are shaping one's perceptions and then considering alternative, more balanced interpretations. For cynics, cognitive reframing offers a way to break the cycle of negative thinking and begin to see people and situations from a more nuanced perspective. It doesn't require abandoning skepticism altogether, but rather, it invites a more flexible and open-minded approach to the beliefs that underpin cynical thinking.

The first step in cognitive reframing is *awareness*. Before one can challenge a belief, it must be recognized. In the case of cynicism, this involves becoming aware of the automatic assumptions we make about people or situations. For instance, when someone offers help or expresses concern, the cynical mind might automatically assume that there is an ulterior motive behind their actions. The first question to ask in this moment is: *Is this assumption based on concrete evidence, or is it merely an automatic thought rooted in past experiences or fears?*

Once the assumption is identified, the next step is to *question its validity*. Are all people motivated by selfishness, or is it possible that some genuinely act out of kindness? Is it true that all attempts at change or reform are doomed to fail, or might there be examples of success and progress in the world that challenge this belief? By questioning these assumptions, individuals can begin to see that their doubts are not necessarily grounded in reality but are instead based on past disappointments or a generalized fear of vulnerability.

Next comes *reframing*, which involves intentionally changing the interpretation of the situation. For example, instead of assuming that someone is offering help to gain favor or control, a person practicing reframing might consider the possibility that this person is genuinely trying to offer support. Rather than viewing a societal initiative as a political stunt, one might acknowledge that, while politics can often be self-serving, there may also be genuine efforts to improve the lives of others. Reframing allows individuals to shift from a perspective of constant mistrust to one of curiosity and openness, where they begin to see the complexity of human motivations and the possibility of goodness even in imperfect systems.

Reframing Personal Beliefs About Society

For cynics, societal beliefs are often shaped by the same doubts and negative assumptions that influence personal relationships. Many cynical individuals view the world as inherently corrupt or unfair, shaped by systems that exist to serve the powerful and exploit the vulnerable. While it is true that society has its flaws and that injustice exists, cognitive reframing encourages a more balanced view. This doesn't mean ignoring societal issues or dismissing the reality of inequality or corruption, but rather acknowledging that society is a complex mix of both positive and negative elements. Reform, progress, and meaningful change do happen, even if they are slow and uneven. Reframing the way we view social systems allows us to engage with the world in a more constructive way, as active participants rather than passive critics.

The Power of Empathy in Reframing

One of the most transformative aspects of cognitive reframing is its ability to foster empathy. Cynics, by nature, often struggle to empathize with others, assuming that people are driven by selfish motives or ulterior agendas. By challenging these assumptions, individuals can begin to open themselves up to a more empathetic understanding of others. Instead of interpreting someone's behavior through a lens of suspicion, they can reframe the situation by considering the person's perspective, motivations, and experiences. This doesn't mean naively assuming that everyone acts with pure intentions, but rather, recognizing that people are complex, multifaceted, and influenced by their own histories and challenges.

Reframing can also help individuals become more empathetic toward themselves. Many cynics have internalized harsh self-judgments, viewing themselves as unworthy of love, success, or happiness. These self-critical beliefs often fuel the broader cynicism they hold toward the world. Cognitive reframing helps challenge these negative self-assessments, encouraging individuals to view themselves with more compassion. Instead of seeing past failures or disappointments as evidence of personal inadequacy, they can reframe them as part of the human experience—moments that offer opportunities for growth, learning, and resilience.

Practical Techniques for Challenging Doubts

- **Reality Check**: When negative or cynical thoughts arise, pause and ask yourself: *Is this thought based on evidence, or is it a generalized belief I've adopted over time?* Try to find real-life examples that contradict your cynical assumptions.
- **Cost-Benefit Analysis**: Examine the emotional cost of holding onto a cynical belief. Ask yourself how this belief is

serving you. Is it protecting you from pain, or is it isolating you from potential joy, connection, and growth? Consider what it might cost you in the long run to continue thinking this way.

- **Ask Open-Ended Questions**: Instead of making snap judgments about people or situations, try asking open-ended questions that encourage curiosity. For instance, instead of assuming someone is acting out of selfishness, ask, *What might this person's motivations be?* or *What else could be driving this behavior?*

- **Perspective Shifting**: When confronted with a difficult situation or relationship, consciously shift your perspective. Try to see the situation from the other person's point of view. What might their fears, desires, or challenges be? What would you want from others if you were in their shoes?

Conclusion

Challenging doubts and reframing cynical beliefs is a gradual process, one that requires patience, self-awareness, and a willingness to engage with discomfort. It's not about rejecting skepticism or becoming blindly optimistic but rather about developing a more balanced, open, and empathetic way of interacting with the world. Through techniques like cognitive reframing, individuals can begin to dismantle the protective walls of cynicism, replacing them with a more grounded and authentic perspective that allows for genuine connection, growth, and emotional freedom.

Embracing Vulnerability

Embracing vulnerability is perhaps one of the most counterintuitive yet profoundly transformative actions a person can take, especially for those who have been trapped in the defensive shell of cynicism. Cynics often perceive vulnerability as a weakness—a flaw that exposes them to the pain of disappointment, rejection, or betrayal. This belief stems from a deeply ingrained fear that vulnerability opens the door to hurt and disappointment. Over time, this fear creates a hardened shell, one that shields the individual from emotional intimacy, connection, and the richness of human experience. However, embracing vulnerability is not about opening oneself up to inevitable harm or rejection. Rather, it is a pathway to personal growth, emotional healing, and a more authentic, meaningful engagement with the world.

The Paradox of Vulnerability: Strength Through Openness

At its core, vulnerability involves the willingness to show up in the world as one truly is—to expose the parts of oneself that are raw, uncertain, or imperfect. It is the courage to be emotionally open, to take risks in relationships, and to trust others despite the possibility of pain. Vulnerability often feels like a threat to cynics because it directly contradicts the protective mechanisms that have been put in place over the years. For a cynic, trust is often seen as a dangerous gamble, and openness is viewed as an invitation for hurt. The belief that "If I don't let anyone in, I won't get hurt" seems like a logical way to preserve emotional safety.

However, what many fail to realize is that true emotional safety does not come from shutting oneself off from the world—it comes from learning to navigate life with openness, even when it feels risky. When we open ourselves up to vulnerability, we give ourselves the opportunity to experience life more fully. We allow ourselves to be seen in our most authentic form, to express our true feelings, and to receive love and support without the filter of cynicism. Paradoxically, it is through vulnerability that we find true strength. Vulnerability is not about being weak; it is about being courageous enough to face the unknown, to take risks without knowing the outcome, and to engage deeply with others despite the possibility of being hurt.

The Role of Vulnerability in Personal Growth

The process of embracing vulnerability is inherently tied to personal growth. Growth—whether emotional, psychological, or relational—requires us to step outside our comfort zones, to challenge long-held beliefs and assumptions, and to take risks that may lead to failure or disappointment. For cynics, personal growth can often feel like a double-edged sword: on one hand, they long for change, for deeper connections, and for a sense of fulfillment; but on the other hand, they fear that embracing those desires will only lead to further pain. This fear of vulnerability creates a significant barrier to growth, trapping individuals in a cycle of emotional detachment and self-protection.

To break free from this cycle, one must learn to approach vulnerability not as a liability but as an opportunity. When we allow ourselves to be vulnerable, we give ourselves the space to learn from our experiences, to heal from past wounds, and to build stronger, more resilient emotional foundations. Vulnerability is the key that unlocks self-awareness and self-acceptance. It is through vulnerability that we come to understand our true desires, our fears, and our emotional needs. Rather than viewing vulnerability as a weakness to be avoided, we can learn to see it as a necessary component of personal transformation.

Healing Through Connection

One of the most powerful aspects of vulnerability is its ability to foster connection with others. Human beings are social creatures, and we thrive on deep, meaningful relationships. However, these relationships cannot form if we remain locked in a state of emotional guardedness. When we allow ourselves to be vulnerable, we invite others to see us for who we truly are, imperfections and all. This openness not only deepens our relationships but also encourages others to be vulnerable in return, creating a cycle of trust and mutual support.

In many ways, vulnerability is the antidote to isolation. Cynicism, by its nature, creates emotional walls that keep others at a distance. The belief that "people cannot be trusted" or "no one genuinely cares" fosters a sense of alienation. But when we embrace vulnerability, we take down these walls, opening the door to authentic connection. The act of sharing our true selves—our fears, hopes, and insecurities—can be incredibly liberating. It not only helps us feel seen and understood but also allows us to see others more clearly, without the distortions created by cynicism. Through vulnerability, we form the bonds that provide emotional support, encouragement, and love—bonds that are essential for healing and growth.

Releasing the Grip of the Past

Cynicism is often rooted in past disappointments, betrayals, or heartaches. The fear of future hurt is built upon the emotional scars of the past. Embracing vulnerability involves confronting these past wounds and learning to release their hold on our present selves. When we remain closed off from the world, we unknowingly allow past experiences to dictate our current behaviors and beliefs. We let the pain of past betrayals or failures continue to shape how we view relationships and the world at large. Vulnerability, however, offers a path to healing. By confronting our fears and opening ourselves up to new experiences, we allow ourselves the opportunity to let go of old hurts. It's through vulnerability that we can make peace with the past and, in doing so, free ourselves from its emotional grip.

Vulnerability as Empowerment

Ultimately, embracing vulnerability is an act of empowerment. It's a declaration that, despite the potential for pain, we choose to live fully, to engage deeply, and to trust that our capacity for growth and connection is greater than our fear of being hurt. It is through vulnerability that we regain a sense of agency over our lives. Instead of being driven by a need to control or protect ourselves from pain, we learn to face uncertainty with courage, to accept our own imperfections, and to embrace the richness of life—flaws, mistakes, and all. Vulnerability, in this sense, becomes a source of strength, not weakness. It is the very foundation of resilience and the key to living a life that is not defined by fear but by openness, growth, and emotional fulfillment.

In the context of deconstructing cynicism, vulnerability is a bridge—a bridge from the emotional isolation of distrust to the warmth of authentic connection, from the stagnation of emotional detachment to the dynamic flow of personal growth. To embrace vulnerability is to embrace life itself, with all its unpredictability, complexity, and beauty. It is the path to healing, self-discovery, and ultimately, a deeper sense of peace and purpose.

Rebuilding Trust in Self and Others

Rebuilding trust, both in oneself and in others, is an essential and transformative step in overcoming cynicism. For those who have been hurt or disillusioned by life, trust becomes a fragile concept—something that may have been broken, betrayed, or lost entirely. Cynicism, with its tendency to view others as self-serving or dishonest, often stems from a profound breakdown in trust, whether it's the result of personal betrayal, societal injustice, or emotional trauma. Rebuilding trust is not an overnight process, nor is it a linear journey. It requires patience, self-compassion, and a willingness to take small but meaningful steps to heal from the past and reengage with the world in a more open and vulnerable way.

Trusting Yourself Again

Before trust can be rebuilt in others, it is crucial to first restore trust in oneself. This means rebuilding confidence in one's judgment, decision-making, and emotional resilience. Cynicism often arises as a response to past mistakes, failed expectations, or betrayals. In these moments, individuals may have internalized a belief that they were wrong to trust others or that they are somehow incapable of making wise choices. This self-doubt reinforces the cynical worldview, where the individual becomes hypercritical of their own decisions and starts to doubt their capacity to discern what is real or authentic.

Restoring trust in oneself begins with *self-forgiveness*. Many cynical individuals are carrying emotional burdens from past disappointments—mistakes they've made, opportunities they let slip by, or relationships that ended painfully. A key step in rebuilding trust is recognizing that everyone, including oneself, is imperfect and that mistakes are part of the human experience. Acknowledge that you are worthy of compassion, both from others and from yourself. Forgiveness is not about excusing or forgetting past wrongs; it's about releasing the emotional weight of those experiences, understanding them as part of your personal growth, and using them as stepping stones toward wisdom.

Another aspect of rebuilding self-trust is setting *healthy boundaries*. When we've been hurt or betrayed in the past, it can be easy to swing between extremes—either becoming overly defensive and shut off from others, or being overly trusting and vulnerable to further harm. The key is to strike a balance: learning to trust your own ability to discern what feels safe, what feels aligned with your values, and what feels right for you. Rebuilding self-trust means being attuned to your own needs, recognizing when you're being overly harsh on yourself, and making decisions that honor your emotional well-being.

Gradually Trusting Others Again

Once trust in oneself has been restored to some degree, the next step is to begin rebuilding trust in others. This is often the most difficult part of the journey, as past betrayals or disappointments have left deep scars that make it challenging to believe that others can be trusted. The process of rebuilding trust in others requires a shift from suspicion to discernment—a shift from assuming the worst in people to cautiously giving them the benefit of the doubt, based on their actions and consistency.

The first step in trusting others again is *taking small risks*. Trust doesn't have to be given all at once; it can be earned gradually over time. Start by trusting people in low-risk situations— perhaps by confiding in a friend about something small and seeing how they respond. Do they listen with empathy and respect? Do they honor your confidentiality? Over time, as you experience these positive interactions, you begin to build evidence that there are trustworthy people in your life. Trust is not a one-size-fits-all concept; some people will earn your trust more quickly, while others may take longer to prove themselves. However, by allowing people to demonstrate their integrity through consistent, respectful actions, you will begin to rebuild your belief that others can be trusted.

Vulnerability is another key component of rebuilding trust in others. While it may seem counterintuitive, allowing yourself to be vulnerable—sharing your thoughts, feelings, and experiences with others—gives them the opportunity to show you that they can handle your emotions with care and respect. It is through these shared experiences of vulnerability that deeper connections are formed, and trust can begin to take root. Vulnerability also teaches you to embrace uncertainty, to acknowledge that not everyone will act in ways that affirm your trust, but that the risk of being hurt is worth the possibility of authentic connection.

Practicing Patience and Discernment

Rebuilding trust in both yourself and others requires patience. Trust is not something that can be rushed; it must be earned and nurtured over time. Part of this patience involves *discernment*—the ability to assess situations and relationships realistically, without slipping into either blind trust or defensive cynicism. Discernment allows you to weigh the trustworthiness of others based on their actions, consistency, and integrity, rather than relying on preconceived assumptions or past hurts. It's about finding a middle ground between being overly skeptical and overly trusting, between being emotionally closed off and recklessly open.

In this process, it's also essential to *manage expectations.* Rebuilding trust does not mean that everyone will meet your standards or that you will never be hurt again. Trust is about acknowledging that people are imperfect and that relationships involve risk, but that risk doesn't have to be paralyzing. By embracing the possibility of disappointment without allowing it to define your worldview, you create space for deeper, more meaningful connections to flourish.

Conclusion: The Healing Power of Trust

The act of rebuilding trust is inherently healing. It's a reclaiming of one's ability to believe in the goodness of others and in the possibility of authentic connection. By trusting yourself first—through self-compassion, forgiveness, and setting boundaries—you lay the foundation for trusting others. Gradually, as you allow people to demonstrate their trustworthiness and as you open yourself to vulnerability, you begin to heal the wounds of the past and create the possibility for richer, more fulfilling relationships.

Trust, once rebuilt, becomes not only a gift to others but also a gift to yourself. It's a step toward liberation from the prison of cynicism, allowing you to engage with the world in a more open, compassionate, and empowered way. Through trust, you reclaim your capacity for joy, for love, and for meaningful connection. It's a process that takes time and effort, but the rewards—a renewed sense of connection, purpose, and emotional resilience—are well worth the journey.

Chapter 5

Navigating the World with Open Eyes

Accepting Imperfection

Cynicism often arises from the belief that the world—and the people within it—should be perfect. It is rooted in a deep frustration with life's inherent unpredictability, its messy nature, and the disappointments that seem to follow us wherever we go. Cynics are frequently caught in a cycle of expecting the worst, seeking fault in others, and deconstructing every situation to reveal hidden flaws or ulterior motives. This worldview, while protective in some ways, creates a heavy emotional burden, one that leaves individuals feeling isolated, disillusioned, and at odds with the world around them.

One of the most powerful and liberating steps toward breaking free from cynicism is accepting that the world is, by its very nature, imperfect. Life, people, and even our best intentions are riddled with flaws and contradictions. Rather than seeing imperfection as something to be avoided or criticized, accepting it can bring a sense of peace and ease that frees us from the constant cycle of disillusionment.

The Gift of Acceptance: Embracing Life's Flaws

The idea of accepting imperfection is paradoxical, yet profoundly freeing. It is not about resigning oneself to a life of mediocrity or apathy; it's about relinquishing the unrealistic expectations of perfection that often fuel cynicism. When we accept that people will disappoint us, that systems will fail us, and that we, too, will make mistakes, we create space for compassion—both for ourselves and for others. This acceptance allows us to see the beauty in the imperfections of life, in the unpredictability of human behavior, and in the flawed yet resilient nature of the world around us.

For example, when we look at a relationship, rather than expecting it to be flawless or devoid of conflict, we begin to appreciate the small moments of connection and growth that happen despite the inevitable misunderstandings and differences. Accepting imperfection means recognizing that no person or relationship can live up to an idealized version of what we want or expect them to be. Instead, it's about finding peace in the reality that relationships are dynamic—they require effort, communication, and a willingness to forgive. By letting go of rigid standards, we can experience the joy and depth that come from accepting others as they are, flaws and all.

Similarly, the imperfections in the world, such as systemic injustices, environmental issues, or political corruption, often fuel cynical beliefs that nothing can ever change or improve. However, accepting that the world will always have its flaws doesn't mean giving up on progress. It means understanding that perfection is an impossible standard. The real beauty of life comes not in striving for a flawless existence but in working toward progress, even when the outcomes are imperfect. Social change, personal growth, and innovation are all messy processes that involve setbacks, failures, and adjustments. By accepting that imperfections are a part of the journey, we are better able to engage in the process of change without becoming discouraged by the inevitable challenges along the way.

Shifting the Lens: From Perfectionism to Compassion

A critical part of embracing imperfection is learning to shift our perspective. Instead of seeing flaws as evidence of failure, we begin to see them as part of the larger narrative of growth and human experience. The cynic often sees imperfection as a reason to withdraw or disengage, but through acceptance, we can shift from a mindset of judgment to one of compassion. This shift does not come easily, especially for those who have been hurt by the imperfections of others or by their own mistakes, but it is necessary for moving beyond cynicism.

Compassion allows us to meet others—and ourselves—where we are, rather than where we think we should be. When we accept that people are inherently imperfect, we can stop expecting them to fulfill all of our emotional needs, and instead, learn to appreciate them for who they are. We can start to see others' flaws not as betrayals but as opportunities for understanding and connection. This mindset shift can drastically improve the way we interact with the world, making us more patient, empathetic, and forgiving.

For example, when we make mistakes, we are often our harshest critics. Cynicism can amplify these feelings of inadequacy, making us feel like failures or frauds. But accepting our own imperfections, and recognizing that failure is an inevitable part of the human experience, allows us to approach ourselves with more compassion. Instead of internalizing our mistakes as proof that we are not enough, we can see them as learning experiences that help us grow. The key is to acknowledge the imperfection without allowing it to define us. This mindset creates space for self-acceptance and allows us to move forward with a renewed sense of purpose and possibility.

The Power of Letting Go: Releasing the Need for Control

Another aspect of embracing imperfection is letting go of the need for control. Cynicism often comes from a place of trying to control outcomes in order to avoid disappointment. When we feel like we cannot trust the world to deliver the results we desire, we may try to manipulate situations or people to ensure that things go the way we think they should. However, this need for control is not only exhausting but also counterproductive. It limits our ability to engage with life in a meaningful way because we become so fixated on achieving perfection that we miss the richness of the present moment.

By accepting that we cannot control every aspect of life, we free ourselves from the anxiety and stress that come from trying to do so. Accepting imperfection means acknowledging that life will unfold as it does, and that sometimes the most meaningful moments come from the unexpected or the imperfect. This doesn't mean becoming passive or disengaged; it means embracing the ebb and flow of life with a sense of curiosity and openness, knowing that even in the chaos and uncertainty, there is beauty and possibility.

Cultivating Resilience Through Acceptance

One of the most powerful outcomes of embracing imperfection is the cultivation of resilience. Resilience is the ability to bounce back from adversity, to adapt to change, and to persevere in the face of challenges. Cynicism often comes from a place of weariness—a belief that the world is too broken or too flawed to be worth the effort. But when we accept imperfection, we are better equipped to face the hardships of life with grace. Instead of seeing setbacks as confirmation of the world's failure, we begin to view them as opportunities for growth and learning.

Resilience is built on the foundation of acceptance. It is the understanding that we cannot always control the outcome, but we can control how we respond to life's challenges. Acceptance allows us to let go of rigid expectations, to release the need for things to go perfectly, and to embrace the messiness of life as part of the process. This shift in perspective fosters inner strength and encourages a more flexible, open-minded approach to navigating the world.

Conclusion: Finding Peace in Imperfection

In the end, embracing imperfection is about finding peace in the present moment, regardless of how imperfect it may be. Cynicism, with its focus on flaws and faults, keeps us trapped in a cycle of disappointment, disillusionment, and emotional detachment. By accepting that life, people, and even ourselves are inherently imperfect, we can release the weight of unrealistic expectations and begin to engage with the world in a more meaningful and compassionate way. This acceptance does not mean resignation; it means opening ourselves up to the beauty and complexity of life, finding joy in the journey rather than the destination. In learning to accept imperfection, we are free to experience life more fully—without fear, without judgment, and with the full awareness that, despite everything, life is still worth living.

Choosing Optimism Without Naivety

Choosing optimism in the face of a world that often feels fractured and uncertain is one of the most powerful decisions a person can make. Yet, for those who have experienced the sting of disappointment, betrayal, or loss, optimism can feel almost out of reach. Cynicism, by contrast, often becomes a defense mechanism against the vulnerability of hope. Cynics view optimism as naïve or foolish, a form of emotional escapism that invites pain. However, the true path to healing and personal growth lies not in abandoning hope altogether, nor in retreating into a defensive stance of perpetual skepticism. It lies in finding the delicate balance between maintaining a hopeful outlook and acknowledging life's inherent challenges and imperfections. This balance is not only achievable but necessary for those seeking to live a life of fulfillment and authenticity.

The Dangers of Extreme Optimism and Extreme Cynicism

Extreme optimism, often characterized by an unwavering belief that everything will work out perfectly, regardless of circumstances, can be just as harmful as extreme cynicism. It leads to a form of blindness—where one refuses to acknowledge the darker sides of life, the complexities of human behavior, and the realities of the world. Such an outlook is not rooted in genuine hope but in denial, a refusal to accept that things don't always go according to plan and that the world is full of contradictions, struggles, and unfairness. Extreme optimism creates unrealistic expectations, setting people up for disappointment when life inevitably deviates from their idealized vision.

On the other hand, extreme cynicism, while born from a desire to protect oneself from disappointment, closes off the possibility of true connection, joy, and hope. It assumes that people, society, and the world are fundamentally flawed and untrustworthy, leading to a worldview dominated by suspicion, negativity, and resignation. Cynicism denies the possibility of genuine goodness, meaningful relationships, or positive change. By embracing a purely cynical outlook, individuals limit their capacity to experience the full range of human emotions and miss opportunities for personal growth and fulfillment.

A Realistic, Open-Hearted Approach

The key, then, is to find a middle ground—a space where optimism is rooted in a realistic understanding of life's complexities. This approach allows us to maintain an open heart, to hope for the best, and to believe in the potential for goodness in ourselves and others, without falling prey to the idealized, unrealistic notions of pure optimism. It is about *choosing* hope and possibility while staying grounded in the knowledge that challenges and setbacks are an inevitable part of the journey. Optimism, when balanced with realism, provides a foundation for resilience, while also allowing us to embrace life's imperfections and uncertainties without being overwhelmed by them.

A realistic, open-hearted approach starts with accepting that life will never be perfect. We will experience pain, loss, and disappointment along the way. People will let us down, and society will fail to live up to our highest expectations. But that doesn't mean we must abandon hope or embrace cynicism. Instead, we can choose to approach life with a sense of possibility, an openness to connection, and a willingness to take calculated risks, even in the face of uncertainty. Optimism becomes a conscious choice to focus on the good—the moments of kindness, the potential for growth, and the beauty that exists, even amidst the chaos.

The Role of Healthy Skepticism

Choosing optimism without naivety requires a healthy level of skepticism—an ability to critically assess situations, recognize risks, and remain discerning in our judgments. Healthy skepticism allows us to approach life with both an open heart and a protective lens. It involves questioning, but not rejecting, the motivations of others, and considering both the positive and negative aspects of a situation. Healthy skepticism is not about assuming the worst in people or situations, but rather about remaining aware of potential pitfalls while still allowing ourselves to hope and act in ways that align with our values and aspirations.

For instance, in relationships, a person with a realistic, open-hearted approach will acknowledge that not everyone is trustworthy, but they will also be open to the possibility that some relationships can be built on trust, care, and mutual respect. They will not be blinded by idealism, but they will also not close themselves off from the opportunity for genuine connection. They will approach others with cautious optimism—understanding that trust is earned over time, and that vulnerability is both necessary and valuable, even in the face of potential hurt.

Embracing the Process of Change

Choosing optimism also requires a willingness to embrace the *process* of life rather than the destination. It is an acknowledgment that personal growth, healing, and meaningful change take time. Optimism, when balanced with realism, is not about expecting immediate results or perfect outcomes but about holding onto the belief that change is always possible, that progress can be made, and that even in the face of setbacks, we are capable of moving forward. Optimism is about maintaining a sense of direction, a belief in the possibility of better days, without insisting that everything must fall into place perfectly in order to be worthwhile.

By choosing optimism with a healthy dose of skepticism, we allow ourselves to hope for the best while also preparing for the reality of life's challenges. This balance provides the emotional resilience needed to face difficulties without being crushed by them. It empowers us to take risks, pursue dreams, and build meaningful connections without falling into the trap of blind idealism or hardened cynicism.

Conclusion: The Path Forward

Ultimately, the key to choosing optimism without naivety is about reclaiming our agency in how we respond to the world. It is about understanding that while we cannot control every aspect of life, we do have control over our mindset, our outlook, and our choices. By embracing a realistic, open-hearted approach, we free ourselves from the constraints of cynicism and allow ourselves to move through life with a sense of possibility, grounded in the acceptance of imperfection. This approach enables us to navigate the world with open eyes, seeing both its beauty and its flaws, while choosing to focus on the good, the hopeful, and the meaningful. In doing so, we create space for growth, connection, and ultimately, a life that is both authentic and fulfilling.

Developing Emotional Intelligence

Emotional intelligence (EI), often referred to as emotional quotient (EQ), is the ability to recognize, understand, manage, and influence one's own emotions and the emotions of others. It is a skill that, once cultivated, has the power to transform the way we perceive and interact with the world around us. For those who struggle with cynicism, emotional intelligence offers a crucial antidote. Cynicism, at its core, is an emotional defense mechanism—an automatic response to past hurt, disappointment, and betrayal. It is a knee-jerk reaction that stems from the inability or unwillingness to process and manage complex emotions in a healthy way. By developing emotional intelligence, individuals can learn to respond to life's challenges with greater awareness and emotional regulation, preventing the reflexive shift into cynical thinking and opening the door to more positive, productive ways of coping.

The Core Components of Emotional Intelligence

Emotional intelligence is typically divided into five core components: self-awareness, self-regulation, motivation, empathy, and social skills. Each of these components plays a vital role in breaking free from the cycle of cynicism and promoting emotional resilience.

Self-Awareness: Understanding the Root of Cynicism

Self-awareness is the ability to recognize and understand your own emotions and how they affect your thoughts and behavior. It is the first step in combating cynicism because it allows individuals to see the triggers that lead them into a cynical mindset. For example, a person might notice that when they feel betrayed or let down by someone, they immediately resort to negative assumptions about others' intentions. With increased self-awareness, they can begin to recognize these emotional patterns before they spiral into full-blown cynicism. Rather than automatically jumping to the conclusion that "everyone is out to get me," they can pause, reflect, and question whether their assumptions are based on the reality of the situation or on past emotional wounds.

Self-awareness also enables individuals to identify when their emotions are clouding their judgment. Cynics often allow negative feelings—such as frustration, anger, or fear—to dominate their worldview, making it difficult to see situations clearly. By becoming more attuned to their emotional states, they can distinguish between genuine concerns and emotionally-driven distortions of reality. This clarity gives them the opportunity to choose how they respond, rather than reacting reflexively out of bitterness or defensiveness.

Self-Regulation: Managing Emotions to Avoid Knee-Jerk Cynicism

Self-regulation is the ability to manage one's emotions in healthy ways, especially in stressful or challenging situations. Cynicism often arises from the inability to process negative emotions constructively. When life's inevitable disappointments occur, a person with low emotional regulation might quickly default to a cynical attitude, retreating into negativity, anger, or emotional withdrawal. They may shut down emotionally, pushing others away, or they may become excessively critical and judgmental of those around them.

By developing self-regulation, individuals can learn to pause before reacting, taking a moment to reflect on their emotions and consider healthier responses. For example, when faced with a setback or disappointment, instead of immediately assuming that it's an indication of a larger, systemic flaw (in themselves or others), a person can take a step back and assess the situation more calmly. They can ask themselves: "What exactly am I feeling right now? Why am I feeling this way? Is this response serving me, or is it reinforcing a negative pattern of thinking?"

Self-regulation also involves being able to manage stress and anxiety without resorting to negative coping mechanisms, such as withdrawing, blaming others, or becoming overly defensive. By practicing mindfulness, deep breathing, or other relaxation techniques, individuals can stay grounded in the present moment, making it easier to navigate challenging emotions without falling into a cynical mindset.

Motivation: Cultivating a Growth-Oriented Mindset

Motivation, in the context of emotional intelligence, refers to the ability to remain driven and focused on personal goals, even in the face of adversity. For cynics, motivation can be stifled by a belief that efforts are futile, that the world is rigged, or that people cannot be trusted. This often leads to feelings of apathy, resignation, and disengagement from the pursuit of one's goals or dreams.

Developing emotional intelligence involves fostering an internal motivation that is not dependent on external validation or perfection. It means cultivating a growth-oriented mindset, where setbacks are seen as opportunities for learning rather than confirmation of the world's inherent unfairness. When a person with high emotional intelligence faces disappointment, they can acknowledge the setback without internalizing it as a universal truth. They understand that failure is a part of growth and that persistence is key. Rather than becoming cynical about their own abilities or the world's opportunities, they are able to keep moving forward with optimism, resilience, and a sense of purpose.

Empathy: Connecting with Others Without Judgment

Empathy, the ability to understand and share the feelings of others, is one of the most transformative aspects of emotional intelligence. It allows individuals to move beyond their own narrow perspectives and connect with others on a deeper level, fostering compassion and understanding. Cynicism often arises from a lack of empathy—seeing others as self-serving or inherently untrustworthy. This lack of empathy reinforces the belief that people cannot be relied upon or that society is fundamentally flawed.

When we develop empathy, we begin to see others not as objects to be mistrusted, but as complex human beings with their own fears, desires, and struggles. Instead of assuming that someone's actions are motivated by selfishness or malice, we take the time to consider their perspective. This does not mean abandoning healthy skepticism or being overly naïve; rather, it means cultivating a sense of openness to others, allowing room for nuance and understanding. By actively listening, asking questions, and attempting to see the world through another person's eyes, we can foster deeper connections and move beyond the isolation that cynicism often brings.

Social Skills: Navigating Relationships with Authenticity

Finally, social skills—the ability to build and maintain healthy, positive relationships—are essential to overcoming cynicism. Cynics often struggle with forming deep, authentic connections because they are preoccupied with the potential for betrayal, disappointment, or rejection. They may push people away or sabotage relationships before they can be hurt.

Developing social skills allows individuals to navigate these fears in a healthier way, building trust and rapport with others while also protecting their own emotional boundaries.

Strong social skills are grounded in emotional intelligence. When we are aware of our emotions and can regulate them effectively, we are better able to communicate openly, manage conflict, and build collaborative, positive relationships. We are more attuned to the needs and emotions of others, and we can engage in relationships without the constant suspicion or defensiveness that often accompanies a cynical outlook. Instead of viewing others as potential sources of harm, we begin to see them as partners in the shared human experience, capable of both imperfection and growth.

The Transformation Through Emotional Intelligence

Developing emotional intelligence is a process that requires commitment, self-reflection, and practice. It is not a quick fix but a lifelong journey of learning to navigate one's inner world with greater awareness and compassion. For those struggling with cynicism, emotional intelligence offers the key to breaking free from the cycle of negativity and isolation. By cultivating self-awareness, self-regulation, motivation, empathy, and social skills, individuals can begin to respond to life's challenges not with automatic defensiveness or distrust, but with openness, resilience, and a more balanced, nuanced understanding of the world and the people around them. Emotional intelligence does not erase the complexities of life or the possibility of disappointment, but it empowers individuals to meet these challenges with grace, emotional resilience, and a deeper connection to their own humanity.

Practicing Empathy and Compassion

Empathy and compassion are not just virtues to be extended to others; they are essential components of emotional healing and personal growth, especially for those who have fallen into the trap of cynicism. Cynicism, by its nature, is a defense mechanism that arises from emotional pain, disappointment, and the fear of being hurt again. It leads to a worldview where trust is withheld, emotions are suppressed, and vulnerability is viewed as a weakness. To move beyond this closed-off, defensive posture and reclaim a fuller, more meaningful connection with oneself and others, it is essential to practice empathy and compassion—first towards oneself, and then toward others.

The Role of Empathy in Overcoming Cynicism

Empathy is the ability to understand and share the feelings of another person. It involves putting oneself in someone else's shoes, seeing the world through their eyes, and experiencing their emotions. For cynics, empathy may be difficult because of the core belief that most people are selfish, self-serving, or manipulative. This worldview can cause cynics to dismiss the emotions or intentions of others, often assuming the worst and refusing to engage with people on a deeper, more human level. However, the practice of empathy—actively attempting to understand others' experiences, struggles, and emotional states—can begin to chip away at the walls of cynicism.

When we empathize with others, we begin to see them not as adversaries or sources of potential harm but as human beings navigating their own challenges. Instead of focusing on perceived flaws or motives, empathy invites us to view others with curiosity, patience, and understanding. For instance, rather than assuming that someone's helpful gesture is an attempt to manipulate, empathy allows us to consider that the person may simply be trying to offer support, based on their own feelings of kindness or compassion. By choosing to engage with others in this way, we open ourselves to more positive and authentic interactions, which gradually counters the negative, distrustful beliefs at the heart of cynicism.

Empathy also broadens our perspective. It helps us recognize that everyone—whether a friend, stranger, or even an adversary—is shaped by their own life experiences, their own joys, fears, and struggles. By fostering this understanding, empathy makes us less likely to judge others too harshly or too quickly. This shift in perspective allows us to connect with others in a deeper, more genuine way, paving the path for meaningful relationships and a more balanced, open-hearted outlook on life.

Compassion: A Healing Force for Cynicism

While empathy allows us to understand the emotions of others, compassion goes one step further—it involves feeling a desire to alleviate the suffering of others and acting on that desire. Compassion is an emotional response that moves us to offer care, kindness, and support when we recognize another's pain. For cynics, compassion may initially feel like a vulnerability, a potential avenue for more disappointment. After all, if they open their hearts to others' pain, might they not eventually be hurt in return? However, what cynics often fail to recognize is that compassion is a transformative power that can also heal the person who practices it. In the act of offering compassion, we soften our own hardened hearts, open ourselves to deeper emotional connections, and find healing for our own wounds.

Compassion starts with *self-compassion*, which is the ability to treat oneself with the same kindness, care, and understanding that one would offer to a friend in distress. Cynics often struggle with self-compassion because they hold themselves to unrealistically high standards, believing that vulnerability or imperfection is a flaw rather than a universal human experience. However, by practicing self-compassion—acknowledging one's own pain and responding with kindness rather than self-criticism or bitterness—we begin to break down the harsh inner narrative that feeds cynicism. It becomes possible to accept that we are all imperfect, that we will experience pain, and that we deserve compassion despite our flaws and mistakes.

In addition to self-compassion, cultivating compassion for others is equally important. This doesn't mean blindly excusing harmful behavior or ignoring patterns of deceit or toxicity, but it does involve recognizing the humanity of others and responding with a willingness to understand rather than judge. When we see someone's hurt, failure, or struggle, instead of dismissing it or using it to fuel our own negative assumptions, we can choose to extend empathy and care. This act of compassion not only helps to heal others, but it also heals us. It reinforces the idea that love, kindness, and connection are not weaknesses to be feared, but strengths that enrich our lives and provide deeper meaning and satisfaction.

Compassionate Action: Moving Beyond Words

The power of empathy and compassion lies not just in feeling for others but in *acting* on those feelings. It is through compassionate action that we can begin to shift from a life dominated by cynicism to one filled with connection, purpose, and fulfillment. Compassionate action can take many forms—offering emotional support to a friend in need, volunteering for a cause we believe in, or simply taking the time to listen without judgment. These acts may seem small, but they create a ripple effect that touches both the giver and the receiver. They also foster a sense of community and shared humanity, which is often missing in the isolated, self-protective worldview of cynicism.

Additionally, compassionate action encourages us to break free from the narrative of *scarcity* that often underpins cynical thinking. Cynicism, in part, stems from the belief that there is a limited supply of goodness, love, or opportunity in the world—that we must guard ourselves from being taken advantage of because others may be out for their own gain. However, when we act with compassion, we tap into the abundance of human connection and kindness. We realize that by offering care to others, we are not depleted, but enriched. There is enough room for everyone to experience love, care, and connection, and by embracing this truth, we start to let go of the fear-driven need for protection that fuels cynicism.

The Healing Power of Empathy and Compassion

Empathy and compassion are healing forces, not just for the recipients of our kindness, but for ourselves. As we learn to see the world with more understanding, to listen with an open heart, and to respond with care, we release the emotional blockages that cynicism has created. These practices allow us to reconnect with our humanity and with the humanity of others, and in doing so, we find our hearts softened and our worldview expanded. Empathy and compassion invite us to see the world not as a place of constant betrayal or disappointment, but as a shared journey where pain, joy, and love intersect in ways that deepen our connections and strengthen our emotional resilience.

By embracing empathy and compassion—first for ourselves, and then for others—we can create a new narrative. We can transform cynicism into a more open, balanced, and ultimately more fulfilling way of living. It is in the act of caring for others, and for ourselves, that we begin to dismantle the walls built by past hurt, and open ourselves to the possibility of a richer, more authentic experience of life. Through empathy and compassion, we not only heal from cynicism, but we also contribute to the healing of the world around us, one act of kindness at a time.

Chapter 6

Moving Forward: A Cynic's Journey to Healing

Shifting Perspective

The journey from cynicism to a more balanced, compassionate worldview is not a quick fix, nor is it always linear. It is a process that requires consistent effort, self-reflection, and the willingness to embrace new ways of thinking and being. Cynicism, as a defense mechanism, may have been a survival strategy in the past, but it no longer serves the same purpose in the healing process. In fact, it stands as a barrier to growth, connection, and emotional fulfillment. Shifting from a mindset of suspicion, negativity, and distrust to one of openness, understanding, and compassion is a transformative journey that involves practical exercises, mindset shifts, and a commitment to emotional healing. Below, we will explore a series of actionable steps to help break free from the grip of cynicism and move toward a more balanced and compassionate way of seeing the world.

1. Practicing Gratitude: Reframing the Lens

One of the most powerful tools for shifting from a cynical perspective to one of optimism and openness is the practice of gratitude. Cynicism often leads to a habit of focusing on what is wrong, broken, or unfair in the world. This negative focus reinforces feelings of helplessness, frustration, and resentment. Gratitude, on the other hand, invites us to shift our attention to the things that are working well, the moments of beauty, kindness, and joy that often go unnoticed in the hustle of daily life.

To begin practicing gratitude, start by setting aside a few minutes each day to reflect on the things you are thankful for. These can be small, everyday occurrences, like a warm cup of coffee in the morning, a conversation with a friend, or a moment of peace during a busy day. The goal is to retrain your brain to notice the positive rather than the negative. For instance, after a difficult conversation or challenging experience, rather than fixating on what went wrong or how others failed you, try to focus on any positive aspects that came out of the situation. Did someone offer help, even in a small way? Was there a lesson to be learned? Did you show up for yourself, despite the challenges?

Over time, this shift in focus helps to change the way you perceive the world. As you become more attuned to the things that are going right, you will naturally start to see the world through a more hopeful and open lens. Gratitude helps to break the cycle of negativity that cynicism thrives on, providing a counterbalance to the constant fear of disappointment and betrayal.

2. Challenging Negative Assumptions: Questioning Cynical Beliefs

Cynicism thrives on assumptions—assumptions that people, society, or the world at large are inherently selfish, corrupt, or untrustworthy. These assumptions are often formed in response to past hurt or emotional trauma, and they become automatic ways of interpreting new information or experiences. To break free from cynicism, it is essential to start questioning these assumptions and replacing them with more balanced, open-minded beliefs.

One practical exercise is to actively challenge your own negative assumptions in real-time. For example, if you find yourself thinking, "People only do good things for selfish reasons," pause and ask yourself: *Is that really true?* Can you think of a time when someone did something kind without expecting anything in return? Perhaps a family member, a friend, or even a stranger showed compassion or generosity in a way that didn't involve any personal gain. By recognizing and challenging your own automatic negative thoughts, you begin to create space for a more nuanced, less cynical view of the world.

Additionally, practice cognitive reframing: when you catch yourself slipping into a cynical thought pattern, try to reframe the situation in a way that acknowledges the complexity of human behavior. For example, instead of assuming someone is being manipulative when they offer help, consider that they might genuinely want to help because they care. If you find yourself thinking "Everything is always unfair," reframe it as, "There are many injustices, but there are also many people working to make the world better." This doesn't mean ignoring the negative or pretending that everything is perfect—it means broadening your perspective and allowing for the possibility that not everything is as bleak as it might seem.

3. Developing Empathy: Walking in Another's Shoes

A key aspect of overcoming cynicism is developing empathy—the ability to understand and share the feelings of another person. Cynics often struggle with empathy because they are conditioned to see others through a lens of suspicion or judgment. Developing empathy, however, requires a conscious effort to let go of these assumptions and open yourself up to the humanity of others.

Start by practicing active listening in your conversations. Rather than focusing on what you want to say or how you can prove a point, focus entirely on the other person. Pay attention to their words, their body language, and the emotions behind their words. Try to understand not just what they are saying, but why they might be saying it. What emotions are driving their behavior? What experiences or struggles might they be going through that influence their perspective?

Empathy also involves giving others the benefit of the doubt. Instead of assuming that someone's actions are selfish or harmful, try to understand their motivations. Perhaps they made a mistake, or maybe they are dealing with personal challenges that you are unaware of. Practicing empathy doesn't mean excusing bad behavior—it means recognizing that everyone is human and deserving of compassion, even if they've let you down in the past.

Another way to develop empathy is by volunteering or engaging in acts of kindness.

Helping others in need can increase your understanding of their struggles, while also fostering a deeper sense of connection and community. Acts of kindness not only benefit the recipient but can also foster a sense of fulfillment and gratitude within you, helping to break down the walls of cynicism.

4. Self-Compassion: Embracing Your Imperfections

In addition to cultivating empathy for others, self-compassion is a critical element of shifting from cynicism to a more open-hearted worldview. Cynicism often stems from a deep fear of vulnerability and a reluctance to accept one's own imperfections. To move forward, it is essential to practice self-compassion—to recognize that you, too, are a work in progress, deserving of kindness, forgiveness, and understanding.

Begin by acknowledging your own emotional wounds and allowing yourself to feel and process them without judgment. Rather than berating yourself for feeling hurt, angry, or disappointed, practice speaking to yourself with the same kindness and understanding you would offer to a friend in distress. Remind yourself that it's okay to be imperfect, to make mistakes, and to experience setbacks. Healing begins when we stop demanding perfection from ourselves and allow room for growth and learning.

Self-compassion also involves letting go of harsh self-criticism and accepting your own humanity. If you find yourself slipping into self-doubt or self-blame, pause and ask: *Would I speak to a friend this way if they were struggling?* Allow yourself to experience self-acceptance, knowing that your worth is not determined by past mistakes or perceived failures. This internal shift creates the emotional foundation for a more balanced perspective on life.

5. Cultivating Hope: Trusting the Possibility of Change

Finally, it's essential to cultivate hope. Cynicism often thrives on a belief that nothing will ever improve—that people will always disappoint us, that the world will remain broken, and that we are powerless to change anything. Hope, on the other hand, is the belief that positive change is possible. It is the trust that, despite the challenges we face, things can improve, and we have the power to contribute to that change.

Cultivating hope doesn't mean ignoring reality or denying the existence of suffering. It means acknowledging the difficulties we face while also recognizing the opportunities for growth, healing, and transformation. Start small—take note of positive changes happening around you, whether in your personal life or in the world at large. Acknowledge the kindness, generosity, and resilience that exist, even in the face of adversity.

By focusing on the potential for positive change, you can shift your perspective and begin to view the future with greater optimism and possibility.

In conclusion, the journey from cynicism to a more balanced, compassionate worldview is a process of transformation. It requires a willingness to question old beliefs, challenge negative assumptions, and embrace new ways of thinking. By practicing gratitude, empathy, self-compassion, and hope, you can begin to heal from the wounds that fuel cynicism and open yourself up to a richer, more connected experience of life. Though the road may not always be easy, each step forward is an opportunity to embrace a more fulfilling, authentic way of being—one that acknowledges life's imperfections but chooses to move forward with hope, compassion, and a deep sense of possibility.

The Role of Self-Reflection

Self-reflection and introspection are essential practices in the journey of overcoming cynicism. Cynicism, as a defense mechanism, often emerges as a way to protect oneself from the pain of disappointment, betrayal, or unmet expectations. However, the very act of closing oneself off emotionally can prevent growth, connection, and healing. To move beyond the negative, distrustful mindset of cynicism, it is crucial to turn inward—to examine the root causes of cynical beliefs, acknowledge the underlying emotional wounds, and explore healthier ways of thinking and being. Self-reflection provides the space to challenge these entrenched thought patterns, gain insight into our motivations, and create a path toward emotional healing.

Through practices such as journaling, meditation, and mindfulness, we can cultivate a deeper understanding of our emotions, behaviors, and thought processes. These practices not only help us identify the sources of our cynicism but also offer powerful tools for shifting our mindset, embracing vulnerability, and cultivating a more compassionate, open-hearted approach to life.

1. Journaling: Exploring the Inner Landscape

Journaling is one of the most effective tools for self-reflection. It offers a private, intimate space where we can confront our thoughts and feelings in a structured yet free-flowing way. For someone dealing with cynicism, journaling can serve as a powerful means of unpacking the negative beliefs and emotional triggers that fuel their worldview.

To begin, start by setting aside time each day to write without judgment or restraint. Allow your thoughts to flow freely onto the page. You may begin by writing about a specific situation or experience that triggered a cynical response—

perhaps a moment of disappointment or betrayal. Explore how you felt in that moment, what assumptions or beliefs arose, and how those emotions have shaped your current perspective on life.

As you write, ask yourself probing questions to explore the root causes of your cynicism. For example:

- What past experiences have contributed to my current distrust of others?
- Are there patterns in my thinking that I notice when I feel disappointed or hurt?
- How might my cynicism be protecting me from vulnerability or emotional pain?
- What beliefs do I hold about people, relationships, or the world that may no longer serve me?

These questions encourage introspection and can help bring unconscious thought patterns to the surface. Over time, journaling allows you to gain clarity on the ways in which cynicism has shaped your perception of the world and opens the door to self-compassion and new perspectives.

2. Meditation: Cultivating Awareness and Emotional Regulation

Meditation is another powerful practice for cultivating self-awareness and emotional intelligence, both of which are crucial for overcoming cynicism. Cynicism often arises as an automatic, reactive response to perceived threats or disappointments. Meditation helps break this cycle by fostering mindfulness—the ability to observe thoughts, emotions, and sensations without becoming attached to them.

Through regular meditation practice, you learn to create emotional distance from your thoughts. Instead of automatically reacting to a situation with skepticism, fear, or negativity, you can observe your emotions and choose how to respond more thoughtfully. This emotional detachment doesn't mean suppressing feelings or denying pain, but rather creating a healthy space where you can process and understand your emotions before allowing them to dictate your actions.

A useful meditation technique for overcoming cynicism is the practice of *mindfulness of thoughts.* In this practice, you observe your thoughts as they arise, acknowledging them without judgment. When a cynical thought appears—such as, "People are always out for themselves" or "Nothing ever goes right"—you acknowledge it, but you don't allow it to control your mindset. Instead, you gently remind yourself that thoughts are not facts; they are transient and often influenced by past experiences. Over time, this practice helps you gain more control over your mental habits, allowing you to respond to life with greater emotional balance and clarity.

Another useful meditation technique is *loving-kindness meditation*, which focuses on cultivating compassion for oneself and others. This practice can help dissolve the harshness of cynicism by promoting empathy and understanding. During loving-kindness meditation, you silently repeat phrases like "May I be happy, may I be safe, may I be healthy, may I live with ease." As you practice on yourself, you gradually extend these wishes of well-being to others, including those with whom you may have conflict or distrust. This simple yet profound practice shifts the focus from a defensive, negative outlook to one of connection, kindness, and goodwill.

3. Mindfulness: Living in the Present Moment

Mindfulness, like meditation, is rooted in the principle of being present in the moment—aware of our thoughts, emotions, and physical sensations without being overwhelmed or consumed by them. For someone struggling with cynicism, mindfulness helps break the pattern of negative thinking and emotional reactivity that often arises from past disappointments or future anxieties.

Cynics are often trapped in a cycle of "catastrophizing"—assuming that bad things will always happen, or that others are always going to let them down. This constant mental rehearsal of worst-case scenarios feeds their cynicism and makes it difficult to enjoy the present moment. Mindfulness practices encourage individuals to focus on the here and now, letting go of worries about the past or future.

A simple mindfulness exercise involves focusing on your breath. Sit in a quiet place and bring your attention to the sensation of your breath entering and leaving your body. Whenever your mind wanders or cynical thoughts arise, gently redirect your attention back to your breath. This exercise helps you stay grounded in the present moment and teaches you to be more aware of your thoughts without becoming entangled in them. Over time, mindfulness helps to diminish the intensity of negative thought patterns and creates space for more positive, balanced thinking.

4. Practicing Compassionate Self-Talk

A critical aspect of self-reflection is how we speak to ourselves—our internal dialogue. Cynics often have a harsh inner critic, one that reinforces negative beliefs about themselves and others. This inner voice may tell them that they're not good enough, that they'll always be let down, or that people are inherently selfish. This kind of self-talk feeds cynicism, perpetuating feelings of insecurity, mistrust, and disillusionment.

To counter this, practice *compassionate self-talk*. This means speaking to yourself with the same kindness, patience, and understanding that you would offer a friend who is struggling. When you catch yourself engaging in negative or cynical thoughts, pause and ask yourself: How would I comfort someone I care about if they were feeling this way? How can I offer myself a kind, nurturing response?

For example, if you feel betrayed by someone, instead of immediately retreating into cynicism with thoughts like, "I knew they would disappoint me," practice offering yourself compassion: "It hurts that this happened, and I'm allowed to feel upset. But I am resilient, and I can move through this." By reframing negative self-talk in a compassionate way, you start to shift your internal narrative, creating space for healing and growth.

Conclusion: The Healing Power of Self-Reflection

Self-reflection, whether through journaling, meditation, mindfulness, or compassionate self-talk, is a foundational tool in overcoming cynicism. By consistently engaging in these practices, you learn to identify the emotional wounds and thought patterns that fuel your cynical worldview. More importantly, you begin to cultivate emotional awareness and self-compassion—two key ingredients for healing.

Through self-reflection, you come to realize that cynicism, while it may have once served as a defense mechanism, no longer serves you in the same way. By creating a safe space for self-exploration and emotional processing, you open the door to a more balanced, compassionate worldview—one where you can embrace vulnerability, trust in yourself and others, and find joy in the imperfections of life. This journey of self-reflection is not about achieving perfection but about learning to navigate life with greater awareness, authenticity, and emotional resilience.

Finding Meaning and Purpose Again

Rediscovering a sense of meaning and purpose after experiencing disillusionment is one of the most profound and necessary steps in healing from cynicism. Cynicism often arises as a response to unmet expectations, broken dreams, or the realization that the world—and the people within it—are not as perfect or as trustworthy as we once hoped. When our beliefs about life, love, success, or fairness are shattered, it can feel as though the very foundation of meaning has crumbled. This disillusionment can leave us feeling lost, apathetic, and detached, unable to find a reason to keep moving forward. The search for meaning becomes clouded by skepticism, and the world appears bleak, devoid of purpose or promise.

However, it is precisely in the wake of disillusionment that the opportunity to rediscover meaning and purpose can be most powerful. The key lies in learning to approach life with a renewed sense of openness, curiosity, and a willingness to embrace new possibilities, even in the face of past disappointments. Finding meaning is not about returning to an idealized version of life but about creating a deeper understanding of one's self, values, and desires—and building a sense of purpose based on authenticity, resilience, and connection.

1. Reframing the Narrative: From Loss to Growth

One of the first steps in rediscovering meaning is to reframe the narrative of past experiences. For many cynics, painful or disillusioning experiences—whether in relationships, career, or personal ambitions—become the defining moments of their lives. These events are often interpreted as proof that the world is unfair or that their hopes were misplaced. However, this interpretation can trap us in a cycle of negativity, where the past defines our present worldview.

To break free from this cycle, it is essential to reframe the way we view past experiences. Instead of seeing them as failures or betrayals, try to view them as opportunities for growth. Every challenge, hardship, or disappointment carries with it the potential for learning, resilience, and personal transformation. For example, a failed relationship may not signify the end of love, but rather a lesson in what you truly need in a partner, or the opportunity to learn more about your own emotional needs. A career setback might teach you to approach work with a deeper sense of purpose, to reassess your true passions, and to pivot toward new opportunities.

Reframing involves shifting the narrative from one of victimhood to one of empowerment. Rather than being defined by what has been lost, you begin to define yourself by how you have grown and what you are capable of achieving in the future. This shift in perspective allows you to move from a state of helplessness and disillusionment to one of resilience and renewal.

2. Exploring Personal Values: What Truly Matters

Cynicism often stems from the realization that societal systems, relationships, or institutions do not live up to our expectations. This can leave us feeling detached from the world around us, as though there is no reliable anchor to hold onto. In this space, rediscovering meaning and purpose involves reconnecting with our personal values—those deeply held beliefs and principles that guide our actions and decisions, regardless of external circumstances.

Take time to reflect on what truly matters to you—what brings you joy, fulfillment, and a sense of alignment with your true self. These values could include love, creativity, connection, freedom, or growth. By reconnecting with these core values, you create a personal compass that guides your decisions, actions, and relationships, even in a world that may sometimes feel chaotic or uncertain.

For example, if your core value is compassion, finding purpose might involve engaging in activities or relationships that allow you to express care and understanding toward others. If creativity is central to your sense of meaning, seeking out artistic or innovative outlets could reignite your passion and provide a sense of direction. Rediscovering meaning doesn't require a grand, life-changing transformation—it can simply be about aligning your daily choices with your deepest values.

3. Cultivating a Growth Mindset: Embracing Change and New Opportunities

A growth mindset is essential for overcoming cynicism and rediscovering purpose. It is the belief that abilities, intelligence, and circumstances can evolve through effort, learning, and perseverance. Cynics often adopt a fixed mindset, believing that life's difficulties are insurmountable, that people cannot change, and that the future is unlikely to offer any new opportunities for growth or fulfillment. This mindset keeps them locked in a state of despair and stagnation.

To break free from this, you must begin to cultivate a growth mindset—one that sees challenges as opportunities to develop, evolve, and learn. This means approaching setbacks not as proof that life is unfair but as valuable lessons that contribute to your ongoing growth. It involves adopting the perspective that you are capable of adapting, changing, and finding new pathways to meaning, even in the face of adversity.

A growth mindset also invites curiosity. Instead of viewing the world through the lens of judgment and skepticism, embrace it with an open heart and mind. Explore new interests, take on challenges, and be willing to fail forward. Whether it's picking up a new skill, pursuing a long-forgotten dream, or simply expanding your knowledge, the act of engaging with life in this way brings a sense of purpose and vitality.

4. Building Connection and Contribution: The Power of Service

One of the most effective ways to rediscover meaning is to reconnect with others and contribute to something greater than oneself. Cynicism often isolates individuals, leading them to withdraw from relationships, communities, and social causes. This isolation can fuel a sense of purposelessness, as humans are inherently social beings who derive meaning from their connections with others.

To find purpose, consider how you can contribute to the lives of others. This might involve volunteering, mentoring, or simply being present for the people around you. When we give of ourselves—whether through acts of kindness, support, or love—we experience a deep sense of fulfillment that transcends our personal struggles. It is through these connections and contributions that we rediscover the value of life, even in its imperfections.

Moreover, contributing to the well-being of others can also create a sense of community and belonging—critical components of a purposeful life. Whether it's engaging in charity work, supporting a cause you believe in, or offering help to a friend in need, these actions foster a sense of meaning that is rooted in connection and shared humanity.

5. Embracing Spirituality or Mindfulness Practices

For some, rediscovering meaning and purpose is inextricably linked to spirituality or mindfulness practices. Whether through organized religion, meditation, or personal philosophies, spirituality provides a framework for understanding life's deeper purpose. It offers a sense of connection to something greater than oneself, a source of strength and guidance during times of uncertainty.

Mindfulness practices, such as meditation or deep breathing, can also help ground us in the present moment, allowing us to cultivate peace and clarity in the face of life's chaos. These practices encourage us to slow down, reflect, and appreciate the small joys that we might otherwise overlook. They help us let go of negative thought patterns and embrace the possibility of change and renewal.

Conclusion: A New Beginning

Rediscovering meaning and purpose after disillusionment is a deeply personal and transformative journey. It requires a willingness to embrace change, challenge old beliefs, and open oneself to new possibilities. While the past may have shaped your perspective, it does not have to define your future. By reframing your experiences, reconnecting with your values, cultivating a growth mindset, and fostering connections with others, you can move beyond cynicism and create a life that is rich with meaning, purpose, and fulfillment. Life may never be perfect, but in embracing its imperfections, you unlock the possibility of a more authentic and vibrant existence.

Forgiveness—Letting Go of the Past

Forgiveness is one of the most powerful and transformative acts a person can undertake, particularly when it comes to healing from cynicism. Cynicism, at its core, is a defense mechanism—a way of protecting oneself from the emotional pain that arises from betrayal, disappointment, or unmet expectations. Over time, these wounds accumulate, often leading to a hardened, distrustful view of the world. Forgiveness, however, offers a path to release the heavy emotional burden of these past hurts. It is a way of freeing oneself from the chains of resentment, anger, and bitterness that keep the past alive in the present. While forgiving others is often seen as an act of compassion, the true power of forgiveness lies in how it liberates *you*—the person who is holding on to the pain.

1. The Weight of Resentment

At first glance, resentment may seem like a natural response to being wronged or hurt. When someone betrays our trust, lies to us, or causes us pain, it is easy to want to hold on to that anger as a form of protection. After all, if we can hold onto our hurt, it feels like we are keeping ourselves safe from further harm. The more we replay the hurt in our minds, the more we seek to justify our anger or resentment, the deeper we embed these emotions into our psyche. Over time, these emotions fester, eroding not only our sense of peace but also our ability to experience joy, connection, and vulnerability.

The weight of resentment is like an anchor, preventing us from moving forward. The longer we cling to past injustices, the more they dictate our worldview. Cynicism is born out of these unresolved emotions; it is the mental and emotional armor we build around ourselves in an effort to protect against future pain. However, this armor, while it may seem protective, also keeps us isolated and emotionally stunted. It prevents us from seeing the world with fresh eyes, from engaging with others authentically, and from embracing new opportunities for growth and connection.

2. The Freedom of Forgiveness

Forgiveness does not mean condoning, excusing, or forgetting the wrongs that have been done to us. It does not mean that the pain we experienced was insignificant or that the other person is absolved of their responsibility. Instead, forgiveness is about *releasing* the hold that the past has on us. It is the act of choosing to no longer allow the actions of others to dictate our emotional reality or define our future. Forgiveness is for *you*—not for the person who wronged you.

When we forgive, we free ourselves from the grip of bitterness and resentment. We stop giving the person who hurt us the power to control our emotions, our mindset, and our outlook on life. Forgiveness allows us to reclaim our emotional energy and redirect it toward healing, growth, and the possibilities of the present moment. It is an act of self-liberation, where we stop allowing the past to have dominion over our thoughts and behaviors. In doing so, we also begin to dismantle the walls of cynicism that have been built around us, making it possible to approach life with a renewed sense of openness, trust, and compassion.

3. Forgiving Yourself: The Path to Self-Compassion

While forgiving others is often seen as the more challenging aspect of forgiveness, forgiving oneself can be just as difficult, if not more so. Cynics, in particular, may carry a heavy burden of self-blame or guilt. Perhaps they feel they were naïve for trusting someone who let them down, or they may blame themselves for not being able to prevent past disappointments. These feelings of inadequacy or self-criticism reinforce a cycle of negative self-talk and self-doubt, making it harder to let go of the past and move forward with a more open and compassionate mindset.

Self-forgiveness is about accepting that you, too, are human. Like everyone else, you have made mistakes, misjudged situations, and suffered the consequences of those errors. But those mistakes do not define your worth or your capacity for growth. Just as you would extend compassion to a friend who is struggling, you must learn to offer the same kindness to yourself. Forgiving yourself means recognizing that you did the best you could with the information and resources you had at the time. It involves letting go of the self-punishment and shame that can arise from perceived failures and instead choosing to embrace the lessons that those experiences have taught you.

In this process of self-forgiveness, it is important to practice self-compassion. Self-compassion involves treating yourself with the same kindness and understanding that you would offer to a loved one who is struggling. It means recognizing that you are not defined by your mistakes or your past, but by your capacity to learn, grow, and change. When we forgive ourselves, we release the weight of guilt and shame that keeps us stuck in a cycle of negative thinking and emotional pain.

4. The Healing Power of Letting Go

Letting go of the past is an ongoing process. It requires patience, vulnerability, and a willingness to face the pain that has been buried for so long. The act of forgiveness—whether it's toward others or oneself—does not erase the past, but it allows us to *move on* from it. It opens the door to healing, allowing us to engage with life in a more genuine, unguarded way.

One of the most important aspects of letting go is acknowledging that holding on to past hurts does not protect us from future pain—it only prolongs our suffering. The more we cling to resentment, the more we allow our past to dictate our present and our future. By forgiving, we reclaim control over our emotional life and begin to create space for new experiences, new relationships, and new ways of thinking. The process of forgiveness can be messy and nonlinear, but it is also one of the most rewarding and liberating journeys we can undertake. It is through forgiveness that we release the chains of cynicism and make room for healing, growth, and renewed connection with ourselves and others.

5. Practical Steps for Forgiveness

While the concept of forgiveness may seem abstract, there are practical steps that can help guide you through the process of letting go:

1. **Acknowledge the Hurt**: The first step in forgiveness is to fully acknowledge the hurt that has been caused. This may require you to relive painful memories and emotions. Don't suppress the feelings; allow yourself to fully experience them. It's only by recognizing the depth of the wound that you can begin to heal.
2. **Express Your Emotions**: Find a safe space to express your emotions—whether through journaling, talking to a trusted friend, or seeking therapy. Verbalizing your feelings helps to release pent-up anger and frustration, preventing them from festering and hardening into cynicism.
3. **Understand the Situation**: Try to gain perspective on the situation. This doesn't mean excusing the behavior of others, but rather seeking to understand the context, motivations, or challenges that may have

led to the hurt. This can help you see the situation more clearly and reduce feelings of personal victimization.

4. **Make a Decision to Forgive**: Forgiveness is a choice, not a feeling. Decide to forgive—not because the other person necessarily deserves it, but because you deserve to be free from the emotional burden of resentment. This decision may take time, but making it is a powerful first step in the healing process.

5. **Release and Let Go**: Once you've made the decision to forgive, work on letting go of the emotional hold that the past has on you. This may involve actively reminding yourself that the past is behind you, and it no longer has control over your present.

6. **Practice Compassion**: Treat yourself with kindness and understanding. Recognize that forgiveness is not a sign of weakness but of strength. Give yourself the time and

space to heal, and trust that letting go will ultimately bring you peace.

Forgiveness is not easy, but it is one of the most profound acts of emotional liberation that you can undertake. It has the power to release you from the past, break the cycle of cynicism, and create the emotional space for growth, connection, and a renewed sense of meaning and purpose. Through forgiveness, you reclaim your power, your peace, and your capacity for joy.

Conclusion

Overcoming cynicism is not a quick fix or a simple choice; it is a process—a journey that unfolds over time. For those who have spent years viewing the world through a lens of skepticism, distrust, or pessimism, the shift toward a more hopeful and compassionate perspective can feel overwhelming. There will be setbacks, moments of doubt, and times when the comfort of cynicism feels easier to cling to than the vulnerability of hope. Yet, it is in this very journey of self-discovery, reflection, and growth that true healing takes place.

It is important to remember that overcoming cynicism is not about achieving some idealized state of perpetual optimism or blind trust in others. Rather, it is about cultivating a *new way of thinking*—one that allows space for both hope and realism, for vulnerability and strength, for compassion and healthy boundaries. The process of shedding layers of disillusionment, doubt, and pain takes time, but with each step forward, we grow closer to becoming our most authentic selves.

The road to growth is marked by small victories: moments of self-awareness, shifts in perspective, breakthroughs in emotional understanding. It is a path that requires self-compassion, the willingness to make mistakes, and the courage to keep going, even when the weight of the past feels heavy. There will be moments of frustration and moments of joy, but with each step, we move closer to a life that is not defined by past hurts or the belief that the world is inherently flawed. Instead, we open ourselves to the possibility that life is both imperfect and beautiful, filled with opportunities for connection, growth, and healing.

As you embark on this journey, remember that it is not a destination you arrive at overnight. It is a lifelong practice—one that requires ongoing commitment, self-reflection, and an openness to change. But as you embrace the process, you will begin to feel a deeper sense of peace, purpose, and connection.

At the heart of overcoming cynicism lies the power of hope. Hope is not naive or unrealistic; it is a belief in the possibility of growth, healing, and change. It is the quiet confidence that, despite the pain we have endured, we can create a better future. Hope is the antidote to cynicism, offering us the strength to look beyond the flaws of the world and see its potential for good, connection, and transformation.

Hope is also deeply intertwined with healing. Healing is not about forgetting or erasing the pain of the past, but about learning to live with it in a way that no longer defines us or dictates how we interact with the world. Healing involves releasing the emotional burden of resentment, regret, and disappointment, and finding a sense of peace in our own lives. It means reclaiming the ability to feel joy, excitement, and love—emotions that cynicism often robs us of.

By choosing hope and committing to healing, we not only transform our own lives but also contribute to the collective well-being of those around us. Healing from cynicism allows us to engage more deeply with others, to approach relationships with empathy and understanding, and to foster a sense of community based on shared vulnerability rather than fear. It is through hope that we begin to see the world not as an enemy, but as a place of possibility, growth, and connection.

The process of healing from cynicism is ongoing, but it is one that brings immense rewards: greater peace of mind, deeper relationships, and a renewed sense of purpose. The more we allow ourselves to hope and heal, the more we become capable of living fully, embracing the ups and downs of life with a sense of acceptance and resilience.

Now that we have explored the nature of cynicism, the reasons behind it, and the steps needed to overcome it, the next crucial step is action. It is easy to read about the possibility of change and feel inspired, but the real transformation happens when we begin to put those ideas into practice.

Start with Self-Reflection: Begin by carving out time for self-reflection. Whether it's through journaling, meditation, or simply sitting in silence, allow yourself the space to explore your emotions, your thoughts, and your past experiences. Acknowledge the moments in your life that have shaped your cynical beliefs and ask yourself whether they still hold power over you today. This is the first step in dismantling old thought patterns and freeing yourself from the grip of negativity.

Challenge Negative Beliefs: Once you have identified the core beliefs that fuel your cynicism, start to challenge them. Question the assumptions you have made about others, about society, and about yourself. Ask yourself whether your views are based on real experiences or whether they are reactions to past pain. Practice cognitive reframing—actively choosing to see situations from a different, more balanced perspective. For example, if you tend to view people's actions through a lens of suspicion, try to see them through the lens of empathy, assuming the best rather than the worst.

Practice Empathy and Compassion: Extend empathy to yourself and to others. Understand that everyone is navigating their own challenges, and that hurt people often hurt others. By practicing compassion, you can begin to break down the barriers of cynicism and rebuild connections with the people around you. This does not mean ignoring red flags or trusting blindly, but rather approaching others with a willingness to understand, to forgive, and to offer kindness.

Embrace Imperfection: Accept that life, people, and situations are imperfect. It is precisely this imperfection that makes life rich and meaningful. Perfectionism and the expectation that everything should go right can fuel cynicism when things inevitably go wrong. Instead, allow yourself to appreciate the beauty of imperfection and to find meaning in the messiness of life.

Take Action: Finally, take actionable steps toward growth. Set small, achievable goals to shift your mindset—whether it's practicing gratitude daily, confronting one of your fears, or taking a chance on vulnerability. Overcoming cynicism is not a matter of big, dramatic changes; it's about consistently making choices that align with your desire for a more open, compassionate, and hopeful way of being.

By following these steps, you can begin to move away from cynicism and toward a life of greater fulfillment, connection, and emotional freedom. The road to healing may not always be easy, but it is always worth it. The choice to heal is the choice to live more authentically, to embrace life with open arms, and to give yourself—and others—the chance to experience the full range of human emotions, from love to joy to hope. It's time to release the chains of cynicism and step into the freedom of a more compassionate, hopeful, and connected life.

Take action today, and embrace the journey of healing. The world is waiting for you to live with open eyes and an open heart.

Printed in Great Britain
by Amazon